STUDY GUIDE:

UNVEILING THE MYSTERY OF THE PROPHETIC

STUDY GUIDE:

UNVEILING THE MYSTERY OF THE PROPHETIC

By Dr. Kevin L. Zadai

Please note that Warrior Notes publishing style capitalizes certain pronouns in Scripture that refer to the Father, Son, and Holy Spirit, which may differ from some publishers' styles. Take note that the name "satan" and related names are not capitalized. We choose not to acknowledge him, even to the point of violating accepted grammatical rules. All emphasis within Scripture quotations is the author's own.

Cover design: Virtually Possible Designs

Warrior Notes Publishing
P O Box 1288
Destrehan, LA 70047

For more information about our school, go to www.warriornotesschool.com. Reach us on the internet: www.Kevinzadai.com

ISBN 13 TP: 978-1-6631-0028-3

Dedication

I dedicate this book to the Lord Jesus Christ. When I died during surgery and met with Jesus on the other side, He insisted that I return to life on the earth and that I help people with their destinies. Because of Jesus' love and concern for people, the Lord has actually chosen to send a person back from death to help everyone who will receive that help so that his or her destiny and purpose is secure in Him. I want You, Lord, to know that when You come to take me to be with You someday, it is my sincere hope that people remember not me, but the revelation of Jesus Christ that You have revealed through me. I want others to know that I am merely being obedient to Your Heavenly calling and mission, which is to reveal Your plan for the fulfillment of the divine destiny for each of God's children.

Acknowledgments

In addition to sharing my story with everyone through the book *Heavenly Visitation: A Guide to the Supernatural,* God has commissioned me to write over fifty books and study guides. Most recently, the Lord gave me the commission to produce this study guide, *Unveiling the Mystery of the Prophetic.* This study guide addresses some of the revelations concerning the areas that Jesus reviewed and revealed to me through the Word of God and by the Spirit of God during several visitations. I want to thank everyone who has encouraged me, assisted me, and prayed for me during the writing of this work. Special thanks to my wonderful wife, Kathi, for her love and dedication to the Lord and me. Thank you to a great staff for the wonderful job editing this book. Special thanks as well to all my friends who know about *Unveiling the Mystery of the Prophetic* and how to operate in this for the next move of God's Spirit!

Contents

Introduction

All Christians are supposed to operate in the gift of prophecy. It is not just reserved for those with the office of the prophet gifting. God wants the body of Christ to move by His Spirit and speak prophetically. There is a demand being placed on us to prophesy to the church body in these last days. We are about to see many people coming into the kingdom of God, and with that, we will see countless people healed and delivered. The Spirit of the Lord is willing, so we need to learn how to prophesy effectively. Jesus taught us to be bold, speak forth and speak to mountains (Mark 11:23). To do that, we use the Spirit of prophecy. When we testify about Jesus, it is the same Spirit. The Spirit of prophecy is the testimony of Jesus (Revelation 19:10)!

CHAPTER 1

Speaking From The Spirit of Prophecy

Pursue love, and earnestly desire the spiritual gifts,
especially that you may prophesy.
—1 Corinthians 14:1 ESV

DISCUSSION:

When developing the gift of prophecy, understand that the Spirit is willing to speak forth what God wants to say. You can't restrict people to prophesy. If we are speaking forth truth, and the Word of God, then we are prophesying. When we testify about Jesus, it is the spirit of prophecy. Even testifying through testimonies about Jesus, you'll feel the Spirit of prophecy come upon you. There's no difference when you're testifying about God or Jesus and the Spirit of prophecy. It's the same Spirit. The same Spirit that testifies is the same Spirit that prophesies.

WHAT IS PROPHECY

- ❖ One of the purposes of prophecy is to speak forth the known will of God. He has a will that He wants to be known. We have thought of prophecy as foretelling; however, most prophecy does not tell the future. That is only a small portion of what prophecy is.

  - Prophecy is speaking forth truth and the will of God.
  - Even if what we prophesy doesn't happen, we still have to say it.
  - We still have to speak to the mountains, even if they don't move.
  - We must keep on speaking.
  - We must keep on prophesying.
  - We must keep saying what God says, even if people don't listen.
  - Even if people don't accept the gospel, we must proclaim it because we will see God's purposes being fulfilled.

Why is it so essential to prophesy even if it doesn't happen or people don't accept it?

____

____

____

____

GOD REVEALS HIS HIDDEN MYSTERIES

❖ **Ephesians 1:8-10 TPT:**

This superabundant grace is already powerfully working in us, releasing all forms of wisdom and practical understanding. And through the revelation of the Anointed One, he unveiled his secret desires to us—the hidden mystery of his long-range plan, which he was delighted to implement from the very beginning of time. And because of God's unfailing purpose, this detailed plan will reign supreme through every period of time until the fulfillment of all the ages finally reaches its climax—when God makes all things new in all of Heaven and earth through Jesus Christ.

- Our Heavenly Father, whom we love and adore, has a plan, purpose, and strategy for this age.
- We play a vital part in what He is doing and wants to do, as this age is closing soon.
- The mysteries of the Spirit are being revealed today, and it will cause you to speak prophetically.
- You are going to speak from the Spirit of prophecy.
- The Spirit of God will come upon you and burn within you, then you will speak forth.

- In its simplest form, prophecy is when you cannot help but speak it out.
- There will be power and an anointing on you when you prophesy.
- There will be an impartation within you that has to come forth.
- God reveals His plan, and He has people speak it.
- Prophecy is partially revelation and partially forth-telling.
- Sometimes it is futuristic. Sometimes it is foretelling.

God will tell you what will come to pass in the future. He sent Jesus to the people of Israel, and Jesus shared many things that God wanted to do, but He said the people wouldn't have it, and they rejected Him. It was not God's will for that to happen, but they did not discern their day of visitation (Luke 19:44).

What is prophecy, and what is its primary purpose?

____

____

____

____

❖ **Ephesians 1:3 NLT:**

All praise to God, the Father of our Lord Jesus Christ, who has blessed us with every spiritual blessing in the heavenly realms because we are united with Christ.

- Here's how you develop the fire inside of you that comes out of your mouth when you prophesy:
- Meditate on Paul's revelation; that God has blessed us, and He is worthy to be praised.
- Knowing you are blessed and praising Him is the easiest way to learn to prophesy.
- When you speak, you are speaking by the Spirit because it is what Heaven is saying.
- God is worthy, and He is worthy to be praised.
- He is the God and Father of our Lord Jesus Christ.
- When you proclaim those two statements, you are implying that Jesus came in the flesh and the Father sent Him.
- The demons do not like it when you acknowledge that Jesus came in the flesh.
- An evil spirit will not acknowledge that because it reveals how they were defeated.

- You can test the demons this way because they will not say Jesus came in the flesh —they were defeated by God becoming flesh and walking among us.
- You have every spiritual blessing given to you.
- Everything that God has in Heaven, He is giving to you.
- You are going to ignite those gifts inside of you.
- The Spirit gives these gifts severally as He wills (1 Corinthians 12:11).
- Paul said that he wished everyone would prophesy (1 Corinthians 14:5).
- Prophecy greatly affects more people because they know what the Spirit is saying in their native language.
- Paul said to desire the greater gifts because everyone gets built up (1 Corinthians 12:31, 14:1).
- We can pray to receive the gift of prophecy and have it.
- We have been given all access to the Heavenly realm through Jesus.

How do you develop the fire inside you to prophesy?

____

____

____

____

PROPHESYING FROM THE HEAVENLY REALM

- When I became a new Christian back in 1980, I asked for the spiritual gifts to be given to me. I prophesy all the time because the Spirit always wants to say something.

    - Everything you say in the Spirit is from the Heavenly realms.
    - If you pray in a tongue, your spirit prays, but your mind is not fruitful (1 Corinthians 14:14).
    - Your mind does not understand what you are saying because prophesying is a spiritual exercise, not a mental exercise.
    - You are praying out the mysteries in another language (1 Corinthians 14:2).
    - You are speaking by the Spirit, in your understanding, and speaking forth in a known language (1 Corinthians 14).
    - Whether you pray in tongues, interpret tongues, have someone else interpret them, or prophesy, it is prophecy.
    - Prophecy is equal to tongues and interpretation.

How do you prophesy from the Heavenly realms?

____

____

____

____

CHOSEN TO BE HOLY

❖ **Ephesians 1:4 NLT:**

Even before he made the world, God loved us and chose us in Christ to be holy and without fault in his eyes.

- You have already been chosen in Christ when you prophesy and speak forth by the Spirit.
- God already knew this before you were born.
- There is more weight in the Spirit when you yield your spirit and mouth to what God is saying and prophesy.
- You are eternally secure with Jesus Christ.
- You are eternally secure if you accept Him and are born again.

❖ You would have to walk away from all of this to lose your salvation, but Jesus would chase you down. He will not let you just walk away.

- You are seated with Christ in the Heavenly realms, and now you can speak from your Spirit from eternity.
- God has already selected us as His own.
- He knows who will serve Him and who will not.
- He gives us a choice, but He already knows ahead of time.
- He selects and chooses all people to come to Him.
- He does not wish that anyone should perish (2 Peter 3:9).
- He plans that everyone will come to Heaven.
- He treats people that way until the very moment they pass away. They are judged according to what they know.

What has God done for you as a guarantee that He loves you?

____

____

____

____

How do you acquire the weightiness of God?

____

____

____

____

When you prophesy, where do you speak from?

____

____

____

____

- ❖ God chose us as His own before the foundations of the world. Then, He made the earth and put man in the garden.

    - God knew all the generations that would ever exist would come forth.
    - He has written books about every person, every name, and anyone that has ever lived.
    - God acted as though they would all serve Him.
    - Paul saw this on the other side. That's why he writes this way in Ephesians.

- God chose us to be Holy. He knew that we would be separate, and He would own us.
- He said that He consecrated and set apart every person for Himself with a purpose. He had these plans.

How has God shown that He knows you?

____

____

____

____

❖ Everyone should hear the gospel and know that their sins are forgiven. God had this in place before He ever made the earth and put mankind on the earth.

- He intended that we would be blameless.
- The whole plan and purpose of the prophetic were to speak forth these truths.
- We are all to be blameless in His sight through the blood of Jesus. It was predetermined before the earth was formed and before people were born.
- Jesus always planned to come back.
- He has redeemed everyone, and the blood of Jesus is enough.

- When you yield to prophecy, remember that everything God has planned must be spoken out. When you proclaim these things, it is foretelling. It is speaking forth the truth. Everyone should prophesy and desire to build people up and bring them to the full knowledge of God.

How are we blameless and how have we been redeemed?

____

____

____

____

What are we to prophesy to people?

____

____

____

____

ADOPTED INTO GOD'S FAMILY

- **Ephesians 1:5 NLT:**

  God decided in advance to adopt us into his own family by bringing us to himself through Jesus Christ. This is what he wanted to do, and it gave him great pleasure.

- God did it in love. He signed the adoption papers. Therefore, we are all adopted into His family.
- When you speak forth the truth and prophesy, you must remember that you are speaking forth that everyone is adopted.
- There is no reason why anyone should go to hell.
- There is no reason why people are not healed.

*** I developed my gift of prophecy by concentrating on how God lovingly predestined and planned out everything in this verse.

❖ If Jesus suffered and died, was tormented, received stripes on His back for our healing and deliverance, and was tormented in hell, why would people not want to accept Him?

- Prophecy speaks forth the truth.
- When you prophesy, it's as though you are the mouthpiece of God.
- When an angel comes and gives the Word of the Lord, he is speaking on behalf of God, and often it is in the first person.
- Prophecy is speaking forth as though it is God speaking.

- Prophecy builds people up, their eyes are opened, and they get saved. That is why it is so essential to prophesy.
- God's intention through Jesus Christ is that we would be adopted and accepted.
- It was His good pleasure and perfect will that this happened.

When you prophesy, what are you essentially doing?

____

____

____

____

PROPHESYING FROM THE OUTFLOW OF GOD

❖ **Ephesians 1:6 NLT:**

So we praise God for the glorious grace he has poured out on us who belong to his dear Son.

- God has poured His grace upon us, so talk about how God is pouring out when you prophesy.
- God is an outflow of giving, and we are to receive.
- Jesus prophesied over Jerusalem the night before He was crucified, "Oh how I've longed to gather you together as a hen

gathers her young, but you would not have it." (Matthew 23:37). You did not discern your day of visitation (Luke 19:44).

- God wants to pour His mercy and grace out and lavish all the benefits on us. He has bestowed them on us freely.
- You are prophesying from that mercy, grace, and outflow God is giving when you prophesy.
- Prophecy is an outflow of God's mercy and grace, and God is giving it out to the hearers.
- It becomes an encouragement to build people up in the unity of the faith.

From where do you prophesy?

____

____

____

____

PROPHESYING OF HIS REDEMPTION FOR MANKIND

❖ **<u>Ephesians 1:7 NLT:</u>**

He is so rich in kindness and grace that he purchased our freedom with the blood of his Son and forgave our sins.

- We have redemption and salvation
- It includes deliverance and healing through the blood.
- When you prophesy, you should mention the blood.
- You should mention redemption, deliverance, and salvation, and talk about forgiveness as being complete.
- Share how God has pardoned us.
- Meditate on this verse so that when you prophesy, the Spirit of God can grab hold of these things.
- You have to understand each of these words.
- Forgiveness is complete in accordance with the riches of His grace. That means there is a superabundance of grace in Heaven, and we will never tap the bottom of that grace or mercy.
- He is an outflow, so it will be from that same outflow when you prophesy.

What should you mention and tell people when you prophesy?

____

____

____

____

CHAPTER 2

Prophesying From the Spirit of Truth

...for prophecy never came by the will of man, but holy men of God spoke as they were moved by the Holy Spirit.
—2 Peter 1:21

DISCUSSION:
Learning how to prophesy is done by meditating on God's truths found in His Word. Once these truths of the Spirit get into your spirit, you can effectively prophesy and bring forth the mysteries of the Spirit. It helps to pull from a biblical vocabulary to express what you are seeing or sensing in the Spirit and bring it to a congregation or someone you meet in the marketplace. They do not have to know Christ or be saved. You can speak by the Spirit of God and prophesy into their lives.

- **Ephesians 1:8 NLT:**

  He has showered his kindness on us, along with all wisdom and understanding.

- To shower means to lavish. Therefore, "He has lavished His kindness on us..."
- To lavish also means "an abundance of outpouring." He is outpouring His kindness, wisdom, and understanding on us.
- Wisdom is the application of knowledge.
- Knowledge is when you are given information. With that information, you will be able to repeat back if tested or provide bullet points, but you might not know enough to teach it.

How has the Father lavished His love on you so that you may prophesy about it?

____

____

____

____

❖ The Spirit wants to take what you have heard and seen and give you understanding so that you can expand upon it.

- You can always tell if you have moved from knowledge into an understanding of spiritual things if you can teach it or explain it to a child.

- Understanding is when you can take and add vocabulary to what you are seeing and hearing in the Spirit, explain it, and teach it precept upon precept.
- The understanding that you gain is practical.
- Allow the Spirit to take the written word in Scripture and expand on it in your meditation time. Then, when you go to speak, you will speak from revelation.

❖ I am prophesying to you as I am teaching you. The same Spirit of prophecy is the same Spirit I am teaching from right now. I am speaking because I have revelation on the words that God wrote in the Word of God.

What's the difference between knowledge, wisdom, and understanding?

____

____

____

____

How can you tell if you have a spiritual understanding?

____

____

____

____

GOD FULFILLS HIS GOOD PLAN

❖ **Ephesians 1:9 NLT:**

God has now revealed to us his mysterious will regarding Christ—which is to fulfill his own good plan.

- God has made known to us or pulled back the veil regarding His will.
- God gave Him the ability and authority to do this for us to see what's behind the veil.
- The hidden mysteries are being revealed in this time.
- It is all to fulfill God's good plan.
- God has shown His intention, His strategy, His secrets, and His timeline for what He wants to do.
- It is all according to His pleasure. He enjoys doing this and is happy and excited about everything He reveals to us.
- He purposed all of this in Christ.
- If you are going to prophesy, you will be speaking forth from God's perspective, which is a will that is no longer a mystery. It has been revealed.
- Jesus was slain before the foundation of the world, and God planned it all before He ever made the Earth.

How has God revealed His will to us?

____

____

____

____

PROPHESYING GOD'S PLAN

❖ **Ephesians 1:10 NLT:**

And this is the plan: At the right time he will bring everything together under the authority of Christ—everything in heaven and on earth.

- When you prophesy and speak by the Spirit, you speak about God's plan.
- You are revealing God's intentions.
- It does not matter how young or old you are.
- You have to prophesy even if people don't accept it.

DISCUSSION:

Jesus went around doing good and healing everyone oppressed of the devil (Acts 10:38), but not everyone was healed. When Jesus went to His hometown, they did not accept Him, and Jesus could not heal anyone there (Mark 6:1-6). There were no big miracles done in His town. He had to go there and fulfill the purpose and plan of God even if people did not accept it. Many people today do not accept Jesus, but that doesn't stop God from having people proclaim Him and prophesy. We still have to speak it anyway.

- ❖ At the right time, God said we are going to bring everything together under the authority of Christ (Ephesians 1:10).

    - Jesus came to the earth, died, went into hell, and rose from the dead.
    - He was seated at the right hand of God, and now at the proper time, everything in Heaven and earth He will bring under Christ.
    - We see a struggle and a war between the physical and the spiritual on earth.
    - There is coming a time where this will culminate, and we will be under the rule and reign of Jesus Christ.
    - Until then, we have to proclaim; "Thy Kingdom come; Thy will be done in earth as it is in heaven" (Matthew 6:9-13 KJV).
    - Fulfillment of the times has to happen.

How are we to prophesy towards God's plan?

____

____

____

____

- ❖ When you prophesy, you are prophesying toward the fulfillment of Heaven coming to earth, and it is progressive.

    - We are prophesying toward what is coming at the end of history, the end of the age and it is a progressive revelation
    - Bringing all things together in Christ, things in Heaven and on the earth. It is going to happen.
    - In Heaven, all the saints who lived have run their race and done everything possible.
    - We are here to accomplish our race. Then when we pass away, we will join everyone in Heaven and cheer the people on that are still here.
    - One day we will all be together. The culmination of the ages will happen, and Heaven and earth will be joined together.
    - Eventually, the Spirit realm will take over. We will still have physical things down here, but it will be a new Heaven and a new earth.

What are we to do while we are here?

____

____

____

____

How does accomplishing our race align with when we prophesy?

____

____

____

____

PROPHESYING OF GOD'S DESTINY

❖ **Ephesians 1:11 NLT:**

Furthermore, because we are united with Christ, we have received an inheritance from God, for he chose us in advance, and he makes everything work out according to his plan.

- The Spirit wants to speak through you as you prophesy to people and groups.
- You will be sharing with them how we as Christians are adopted and receive an inheritance in Christ.
- It will make you want to prophesy to people and tell them that they need to partake of the benefits of being adopted.
- The word study for *inheritance* explains that your inheritance is a destiny in which God claims us as His very own.
- He bought us, and now He owns us.

- The inheritance we receive is that we have a destiny in God's plans for us.
- We've been predestined or chosen to do amazing things in Christ.

When you are prophesying to others, what will you share from Ephesians 1:11 with them?

____

____

____

____

DISCUSSION:

When I was in Heaven, I saw that people go to hell and never get to fulfill all the predestined and chosen things appointed beforehand. They go to hell because they do not understand that everything is already laid out for them. All they needed was to be redeemed. They needed to accept Jesus Christ as Savior and get locked into a trajectory appointed beforehand by God.

- ❖ When you speak to others by the Spirit, God has already written their book (Psalm 139:16), and the angels have been sent to fulfill it.

    - When you prophesy to people, you are getting them on their track in life.

- You are called to get them born again and Spirit-filled.
- Speak from the Spirit to encourage and strengthen them.
- God had a plan and purpose, and it was always in Him.

How will you encourage people and prophesy to them about their eternity?

____

____

____

____

❖ When we receive Jesus as Lord, we are locked in. Then we receive His inheritance, and all that God has predetermined begins to happen in succession, as we are obedient.

- The works He has already laid out for us have been determined and agreed upon with a counsel He has met with in Heaven.
- In Hebrew, it says that everything is working according to a counsel that came together in agreement and wrote out these plans.
- Everything works together according to the counsel and design of His will (Ephesians 1:11).

❖ If you meditate on these points, you will speak forth truth:

- Prophecy is supposed to be at a higher level than it has been.
- Many prophecies come from the soulish realm instead of the Spirit realm. It must come from the Spirit of God.
- When you speak from the Spirit, you will speak profound things from the other realm.
- It will not be fleshy, carnal, or emotional.
- It will be Spirit-led and from the truth.
- It will build people up, put them on track, and unify and mature the body. That is what prophecy does.

How do you know you are prophesying by the Spirit?

____

____

____

____

The five-fold ministry of the church is meant to build up the body in the gifts of the Spirit (Ephesians 4:11-16). God gives these gifts severally as He wills to build up the body (1 Corinthians 12:11).

- God's purpose is established ahead of time, so we need to trust Jesus right now with our future.

  - We can trust Him with our future by doing something about it right now.
  - We connect to the Spirit and yield to Him in our hearts, not our heads, and we put our confidence in Him.
  - We exist because He planned for us to, and His purpose will be revealed.

How do we trust Jesus with our future and plans?

____

____

____

____

PROPHESYING THE SAVIOR

- **Ephesians 1:13 AMP:**

  In Him, you also, when you heard the word of truth, the good news of your salvation, and [as a result] believed in Him, were stamped with the seal of the promised Holy Spirit [the One promised by Christ] as owned *and* protected [by God].

- When speaking to people, you have to get them to come toward you and God.
- You want to win them over in their soul by telling them the truth and allowing God's Spirit to convict them.
- They will get won over in their spirit by His Spirit.
- God has destined you on the earth at this time to go forth and bear fruit. He is talking about the fruit of your lips.
- It is all about speaking forth and encountering the supernatural.
- God wants us to speak forth His will.
- He wants to bring what is in the other realm into this one.
- When we see people get saved, that is fruit.
- When we see answers to prayer, that is fruit.

❖ In John 15:4, It talks about abiding in the vine, which refers to prayer, and Jesus later talks about how you will receive whatever you ask for in prayer because you abide in Him. We have received the word about salvation, and you will see its fruit when you prophesy because you are speaking about salvation.

- The Gentiles received the truth because they heard the good news.
- When you hear the Word of Truth, the good news that God saves you, and you believe in Him —you receive Him.

- When you prophesy, it is the same thing.
- When you prophesy and speak the truth, people will hear the truth, believe the truth, and receive the truth —stamped with the seal of the Spirit, as the promised Holy Spirit is a deposit.

What happens when you prophesy the Word of Truth to people?

____

____

____

____

DISCUSSION:

You can see this with the outpouring of the Holy Spirit and salvation. When you receive the Holy Spirit, you are born again (John 3:1-8). Then you receive the Holy Spirit through the baptism of the Holy Spirit, which is power from on high to be witnesses (Acts 1:8). The Holy Spirit is also a deposit, guaranteeing full payment (2 Corinthians 1:21-22). We receive some of that payment now, and some we haven't received yet, but we will accept the fullness of that payment when we get to Heaven. We are stamped with the seal of the promised Holy Spirit, which means that we are owned and protected by God. When you prophesy, you are proclaiming salvation, protection, and deliverance. By letting the Spirit speak, you reveal to people that you are owned and protected by God.

PROPHESYING THE DEPOSITED INHERITANCE

❖ **Ephesians 1:14 NLT:**

The Spirit is God's guarantee that he will give us the inheritance he promised and that he has purchased us to be his own people. He did this so we would praise and glorify him.

- You have been given a receipt guaranteeing what you have.
- You have essentially received the first installment.
- You have received a pledge or a foretaste of your inheritance, and it is inside of you.
- A deposit has been made, and you need to draw from it and speak forth.
- It is forward-looking; therefore, you will be speaking ahead.
- You are going to build people up to come into the unity of the faith and maturity.
- It is essential to continue and be faithful because you are purchased and owned by God.
- You have a deposit guaranteeing your full payment, and that possession is an inheritance in Heaven.

❖ God wants you to speak forward. The children in the womb, and the prophetic generation coming forth right now, will have this fire to speak. I saw that everyone in these end times would prophesy. I saw that the gift of prophecy will be prevalent everywhere and that the youth will be speaking by the fire and prophesying. It will be like their second language, and it will not be hard for them.

What does the Spirit of God guarantee, and why did He do it?

____

____

____

____

PRAY FOR SPIRITUAL REVELATION

❖ **Ephesians 1:15 NLT:**

Ever since I first heard of your strong faith in the Lord Jesus and your love for God's people everywhere.

- Paul heard of their strong faith and love for people, and he complimented them.
- We need to stay strong in our faith and love for people.
- People are talking about your faith and your love.

❖ **Ephesians 1:16 NLT:**

I have not stopped thanking God for you. I pray for you constantly.

- Paul prayed for people constantly and remembered them in his prayers.

DISCUSSION:

There are people that I pray for daily that I have never met, but I have seen their pictures on social media. It might be years before I meet them. Some I have already met. I receive their prayer requests from social media. I pray and speak God's will over their lives and prophesy in the Spirit from the Word of God. I pray in the Spirit, then in English, and I prophesy and speak the truth over them. You learn how to prophesy in your prayer time when you pray for God's will from the Word over people's lives.

What are the two things that we should stay strong in?

____

____

____

____

HAVING SPIRITUAL WISDOM

❖ **Ephesians 1:17 NLT:**

Asking God, the glorious Father of our Lord Jesus Christ, to give you spiritual wisdom and insight so that you might grow in your knowledge of God.

- There is so much glory going on in the throne room and around the Father.
- Paul prays to the God of glory that He would give you a spirit of wisdom and revelation.
- Wisdom is understanding, and revelation is when your eyes and ears are open, and you have an understanding of what you are seeing and hearing.

❖ In Heaven, I saw the glory of God all around you and the Spirit opening your eyes and ears, bringing you to understanding.

- We often see and hear, but we do not always understand.
- Paul is asking God to grant you a Spirit of wisdom and revelation, and from this insight, we would receive a deep understanding of the personal and intimate knowledge of Him.

- The origin and core of prophecy speak forth the mysteries and truth about Father God.
- When you prophesy, you are speaking forth from the Spirit, but on a higher level than what your understanding is down here.
- You can judge and tell when prophecy is from the soul realm.
- People speak from the soul realm because they have not allowed the Spirit to develop them in their intimacy with God.
- Paul is asking that the Ephesians would have their eyes and ears open to receive deep spiritual insight into the true knowledge of God the Father.
- That is the core of prophecy.

Why do you need to grow in the knowledge of God? In intimacy with God?

____

____

____

____

CHAPTER 3

Speaking Forth The Mysteries

No, the wisdom we speak of is the mystery of God—his plan that was previously hidden, even though he made it for our ultimate glory before the world began.
—1 Corinthians 2:7 NLT

DISCUSSION:
Once you understand prophecy, you will begin to operate in it. The Spirit of God will help you and reveal His wisdom to you. Prophetic insight and operating in prophecy are based on truth, not only on foreknowledge. You cannot just think you will prophesy and tell the future because that is not how prophecy works. Prophecy is telling forth the mysteries from the Spirit into this realm. Prophets have spoken about what God intends to happen, but they do not always come to pass, so it is not just speaking about the future.

It was never God's intention for Adam and Eve to fall, yet they did. God knew they would, but He did not prophesy that mankind would fall—He made provision for it. Jesus did not come to the earth thinking He would fail. He succeeded, but the people did not accept Him. They had Him killed. He never failed because He had God's provision and insight. Paul said that if the powers of the age had known, they never would have crucified the King of Glory (1 Corinthians 2:8). It was hidden.

- The whole idea of prophecy is to reveal the truth, so you cannot go by what the Old Testament prophets did by telling the future.

  - Most of their prophecies spoke forth what God intended, but the people didn't listen to the prophecies, and they were punished.
  - Because of it, they encountered terrible times.
  - For example, look at what happened with Israel in the desert. It was not God's will for them to spend all that time there.
  - It was only a twelve to fourteen-day walk into the Promised Land from where they were in Egypt. Why did it take 40 years?
  - It was because of their disobedience, rebellion, and unbelief.
  - It was not God's fault.
  - It was never God's intention for things to take as long as they do in our lives.
  - We need to mix what we believe with action and implement it by loving God so much that we obey Him (John 14:15 TPT).
  - It is these steps of obedience that cause us to enter in and see the favor of the Lord.
  - What we have to do is prophesy and speak forth these things into this realm.

How do you operate in prophecy, and what is it?

____

____

____

____

Pertaining to prophecy, what can we learn about the Israelites not entering the Promised Land for 40 years, and what prolonged their opportunity?

____

____

____

____

THE GLORIOUS HOPE OF OUR INHERITANCE

- **Ephesians 1:18 NLT:**

  I pray that your hearts will be flooded with light so that you can understand the confident hope he has given to those he called—his holy people who are his rich and glorious inheritance.

  - We, as the body of Christ together, are His inheritance.

- His plan is that we would be large in numbers, built up in maturity and unity, and speak in one accord.
- He provided ministers through the five-fold ministry of church to speak to the body and build us up.
- God has given each person the ability by the Spirit to see, know, and understand how to operate in the Spirit.
- It is not a mystery anymore. God has revealed this to us by His Holy Spirit.
- Paul is praying that the eyes of our heart, the center or core of our being, would be exploded and enlightened with light.
- If you read and study these words, they are very powerful.
- They are there so that you can know the hope to which you have been called.
- God has called and chosen you.

Why has God filled our hearts with light? As His holy people, how are we rich?

____

____

____

____

- You might be identifying with how you are feeling right now or how you are being treated. However, at the very core, the center, you will be flooded with light, which will cause you to have understanding.

    - You will not be guessing.
    - You will not have to wait for a feeling.
    - When you prophesy, you are prophesying from knowing.
    - You are prophesying from the fire and cherishing all the hope you have been given.
    - That is what the Spirit would say. He has good news, and He wants to say these things out loud.
    - The hope to which you have been called is the expectation that there will be a divine guarantee fulfilled.
    - It has to do with the hope that you will receive your inheritance.

Where do we prophesy from?

____

____

____

____

❖ When you prophesy forward, you are pushing everyone toward receiving their inheritance.

- It brings hope, and that is what the Lord is praying for people right now.
- We want to speak prophetic utterances over people; that they would have this hope, to see, cherish, and know it in their inner being.
- As a reward, there is a storehouse in Heaven, and it is more than we could ever imagine.
- Our inheritance is there, and you speak and prophesy from that place.
- You can practice this by speaking forth that glorious inheritance.
- When you meditate and concentrate on Ephesians 1:18, it will ignite in you.

Why do we prophesy forward?

____

____

____

____

- You are supposed to be prophesying because you are leading people into a confident hope and expectation where they can grasp that they have this inheritance.

    - When people come together in a service, they want to hear the good news.
    - They want to hear what the Spirit is saying.
    - The Spirit is saying, "I am going to flood your inner core with light, and I will show you the hope to which you have been called; the glorious inheritance in the saints."

UNDERSTANDING THE GREATNESS OF GODS POWER

- **Ephesians 1:19-20 NLT:**

  I also pray that you will understand the incredible greatness of God's power for us who believe him. This is the same mighty power that raised Christ from the dead and seated him in the place of honor at God's right hand in the heavenly realms.

    - Paul is praying that we as believers would understand the incredible greatness of God's power.
    - That power is the resurrection power that rose Jesus from the dead.

- In the Greek definition, "God's power" is considered active spiritual power toward we who believe. It is in accordance with the mighty strength that He produced in Christ.
- The meaning of "incredible greatness" if you look it up and do the word study means immeasurable and unlimited. The Spirit wants to say this to the body.
- The way you prophesy is with the same power that took you and placed you at the right hand of God and seated you with Christ in the Heavenly realms (Ephesians 2:6).
- You have been raised, and you died with Him.
- Paul said this same power that rose Jesus from the dead is dwelling in us.
- What the Holy Spirit produced in Jesus; He is producing in us.
- The same power that rose Jesus from the dead is the same power that you prophesy from. The source is already in you.
- Paul, in these verses, is praying for the Ephesians, that they would be seated with Him and would know that the Heavenly realms are their new home.

Explain the power that you prophesy from.

____

____

____

____

HE IS ABOVE ALL

❖ **<u>Ephesians 1:21 NLT:</u>**

Now he is far above any ruler or authority or power or leader or anything else—not only in this world but also in the world to come.

- In this verse, Paul reveals more of what he saw when he was caught up with the Lord and given revelation.
- God is far above any authority.
- Jesus is seated on the throne at the right hand of the Father, and we are seated with Him.
- We are heirs of God and co-heirs with Jesus, and this is the epitome of the authority that we have in Him.
- When you prophesy and speak forth, you have to speak from the throne, and you have to prophesy from being seated with Him.
- It is the only way that you are going to deal with the demonic.
- The only way that you will see demons leave is by speaking from this place where they are defeated.
- When you read it in the Greek language, it says, He is far above every ruler, far above all authority, far above all power and dominion.

What does Ephesians 1:21 have to do with you prophesying?

____

____

____

____

- ❖ Paul, in Ephesians six, talks about the different echelons of spiritual wickedness. Paul mentions the different levels here, "Far above authorities, powers, dominions, angelic or human. Far above every name, every title that could be conferred, not only in this age, but in the one to come, and we are above them as well because we are seated with Him."

    - If you concentrate and meditate on this verse, it will cause you to see, hear and understand at a higher level.
    - Then you will speak from that level and from that place.
    - It will change the atmosphere wherever you go and impact many people.

DISCUSSION:

I used to shift atmospheres when I worked for the airline, and now it happens in our meetings. We prophesy to thousands of people. Not only that, but there are often over ten thousand people watching online sometimes, and within a week, thirty to forty thousand people have seen it. That is why it is so important that we all prophesy from this high level in the Heavenly realms at the right hand of God, seated with Christ in the throne room. That's where we need to speak from.

What gives you the ability to shift atmospheres wherever you go?

____

____

____

____

How do you defeat the enemy every time you prophesy?

____

____

____

____

CHRIST IS THE HEAD

❖ **Ephesians 1:22 NLT:**

God has put all things under the authority of Christ and has made him head over all things for the benefit of the church.

- We prophesy because God has given us this authority and has established it at the throne and placed Christ there.

- Christ took us to the throne and redeemed us, so now we have the benefit of being heirs and co-heirs with Jesus.
- Every realm is under subjection to God's authority, and it is under Christ's feet for the benefit of the church.
- When you prophesy, you are benefiting the whole church.
- When you prophesy, you are building them up
- God is the supreme authority, and He has made Christ over all things for the benefit of the church, so when you prophesy, you are fulfilling the next step.

What happens when you build up and prophesy to the church?

____

____

____

____

❖ Jesus is seated at the right hand of God, and then He gives the keys of death, hell, and the grave to the church.

- He gives the authority to the church
- Now He is waiting for His enemies to become His footstool through the church (Hebrews 10:13).
- The church is now the Ministry of Jesus on the earth.

- Jesus is the head, and we are the representation on the earth.
- This church, this mystery, is not a church building or denomination. It is the Ecclesia.
- The whole church all over the world are people that are born again and tied together by the Spirit of God.

What unites the body of believers?

____

____

____

____

THE CHURCH IS FULL AND COMPLETE

❖ **Ephesians 1:23 NLT:**

And the Church is his body; it is made full and complete by Christ, who fills all things everywhere with himself.

- Christ's fullness causes us to be complete.
- Even though we see the body of believers in different areas, denominations, and divisions of the world, there is a remnant tied together in the Spirit.

- They all believe in the gospel.
- They all preach the uncompromising Word of God.
- They believe in the Holy Spirit, the miracles of Jesus Christ, and continuing the ministry of Jesus until He comes.
- Some religious people do not believe the whole gospel.
- They don't honor the Holy Spirit or the message of the gospel, such as deliverance, healing, raising the dead, or Jubilee, which is the forgiveness of sin and debt.
- The inheritance that we have now is more than enough.
- All things we need for life and Godliness have been given to us, and we can be partakers of the divine nature (2 Peter 1:3-4).
- Being a partaker of the divine nature allows God to seat us in the Heavenly realms and take a portion from our glorious inheritance, and we live out of that.
- The same power that rose Jesus from the dead is quickening our mortal bodies so we can have all of this.

How is the body of believers made full and complete?

____

____

____

____

- As you yield to the Spirit and meditate on the prayer in Ephesians 1:17-23, you will begin to acquire wisdom, and you need to know these four things:

    - The hope to which you have been called.
    - The glorious inheritance that you have in the saints.
    - The unlimited greatness of God.
    - The resurrection power that rose Jesus from the dead.

- Ask the Holy Spirit to flood you with light; that you may know the hope to which you have been called, and that you may see and prophesy.

    - The renewing of your mind is transforming you, and your spirit is born again
    - Take what God is saying and allow the Holy Spirit to apply it in your life.
    - Look at Scripture as personal prophecy.
    - Scripture is prophesying to you and telling you the truth.
    - As your spirit develops and you gain confidence and understanding, it will ignite a fire in you so that there is an abundance within you.

- Then you can speak forth to others by the revelation of the Holy Spirit, and that revelation will ignite you from within.
- You will begin to prophesy to yourself because you can have everything that is in Scripture.
- As you speak the Word aloud, it causes everything to clear in the spirit around you.
- You will clean out the area and notice the demonic will get pushed back.
- There will be times you will feel freedom because you are prophesying.

Why would you want to be flooded with light?

____

____

____

____

Why is meditating on Scripture effective for prophecy?

____

____

____

____

- As you prophesy and proclaim aloud, the demons will back off and get pushed back. They will get pushed back because they are not occupying your life anymore, and you will see things break open.

  - That is when people begin to see their healing and financial provision come.
  - You will see people who were once demonically inspired have no demonic present anymore. The demonic gets pushed back because you have been prophesying.
  - People will behave better because the demonic presence is gone.
  - You will receive deliverance and financial provision.
  - Relationships will be healed because when you prophesy from the spirit realm, it causes the enemies that you cannot see to be pushed back.
  - It will feel like God's favoring you, but what is really happening is you have done what is proper. This is what you are supposed to be doing.

How does the enemy get pushed back?

____

____

____

____

- I found out when I was in Heaven that I was waiting to be given permission for something that I was already allowed to do. By prophesying the truth in Scripture about the mysteries being revealed, I was able to do it.

  - The purpose of prophecy is to push back the darkness.
  - It is to bring the whole body to a level of maturity.
  - Paul referred to the Corinthians as carnal, even though they had all the gifts of Spirit operating in the services.
  - He could not even address them as spiritual because they were mere babies.
  - They should have been on meat, but they were on milk (1 Corinthians 3:1-2).
  - The people were not operating in the Spirit. They were carnal.
  - They could have all these things happening in the services, but they were not able to be Spirit ruled.
  - They were flesh ruled, and this is the case today.

What is the purpose of prophecy?

____

____

____

____

- We cannot deal with things correctly when they go wrong because we are in a broken world. If we are not in the Spirit, we will not process it properly.

    - When we process things by the flesh and our own understanding, we get into trouble.
    - The divine mystery revealed by Paul is Christ in us—the hope of glory (Colossians 1:27).
    - That is the hope of the inheritance.
    - Everything you prophesy should be pushing people forward and building them up.
    - Once you establish your authority in the Spirit and the demons get pushed back, you will see the favor of the Lord come in.
    - Prophesy to people and friends and tell them of the same truth.
    - When they hear it, they can mix it with faith, then they will learn how to do it, and before you know it, a group of people will have pushed back the enemy. They will begin to see the favor of God.

Why is it imperative to remain in the Spirit and build yourself up?

____

____

____

____

- Local bodies are formed through a group of people that get into a flow of the Holy Spirit, and they call it revival, and revival breaks out.

    - Revival comes because the spirits that were in that territory get completely pushed back.
    - There is a flow and an open Heaven.
    - The body of believers is supposed to be the most powerful entity on the earth
    - We are the ones with the most authority and the most favor, so we have to exercise it and live it.

How does your authority affect everyone around you?

____

____

____

____

CHAPTER 4

Understanding The Prophetic

"The Spirit of the Lord spoke by me, and
His word was on my tongue."
—2 Samuel 23:2

DISCUSSION:

To understand and speak prophecy at a high level, it takes yielding to the Spirit and speaking to your environment from the Heavenly realm. It pushes back the demonic, and then the favor of God will come in a greater way.

❖ **1 Corinthians 2:1 NLT:**

When I first came to you, dear brothers and sisters, I didn't use lofty words and impressive wisdom to tell you God's secret plan.

- There is a plan of Salvation, a plan of restoration, and a mystery that is being revealed in this end time.

- That means there is a culmination where all the powers that be will be judged, and the family in Heaven and earth will be joined together.
- The wisdom that Paul is proclaiming is not from worldly wisdom.
- When he came to the Corinthians, he told them that he wasn't speaking impressive words or proclaiming to be an excellent public speaker.
- He explained that the wisdom he spoke from is not of this world.
- As for prophecy, you cannot speak from the world or the mindset of the world.
- Prophecy comes from the Spirit of God.

From what standpoint is Paul speaking to the Corinthians?

____

____

____

____

SPEAKING FROM THE SPIRIT

❖ **1 Corinthians 2:2-3 NLT:**

For I decided that while I was with you I would forget everything except Jesus Christ, the one who was crucified. I came to you in weakness—timid and trembling.

- Paul decided that he would not know anything else except that Jesus was the Christ, the Messiah, and He was crucified.
- Jesus was the substitution. He died, but He was buried and rose from the dead. It is all about His death, burial, and resurrection.
- Paul said that he came to them in weakness, not with lofty words but in the power of the Spirit. He came to them timid and trembling.
- There is a humility that comes with walking in the prophetic and speaking forth from the Spirit.
- Paul did not speak from his mind but was confident and full of resurrection power.

How is it possible that Paul came to them in weakness and timidity, yet he was powerful in Spirit?

____

____

____

____

THE POWER OF THE HOLY SPIRIT

❖ **1 Corinthians 2:4 NLT:**

And my message and my preaching were very plain. Rather than using clever and persuasive speeches, I relied only on the power of the Holy Spirit.

- When you prophesy, you must stay humble and picture yourself being connected to the river of life flowing out of you through your mouth.
- When you prophesy, picture the rivers of living water coming forth from your heart, forming words while yielding to the Spirit.
- Your mind does not think about anything you are saying because it is not participating.
- When you speak in tongues, your mind does not participate because you speak another language.
- When you prophesy, it comes from the same Spirit as tongues, so your mind does not participate in that (1 Corinthians 14:14).
- Even if you can hear and understand what you are saying in your known language, the Spirit is using you and speaking through you.
- You do not necessarily hear what you are saying because you are being used of the Lord.

Explain how speaking from the Spirit is different than speaking from the flesh?

____

____

____

____

❖ I usually have to be told what I prophesied. I don't always remember what I said because my mind is shut off.

- When you prophesy, you are prophesying by the power of the Holy Spirit, which means you are relying on Him.
- In the message that Paul delivered to the Corinthians, he did in demonstration of the Holy Spirit and the power of God operating through him.
- He was persuading people through the Spirit, so he was not appealing to their flesh or appealing to their minds.
- He was appealing to their spirit. It is Spirit to spirit.
- When you prophesy, you are coming from timidness or weakness in the flesh, but you are coming in the power of the Holy Spirit and speaking powerful spiritual words from the other realm.
- You are speaking from the rivers of living water coming up from within.

- The wisdom and knowledge in your mind and flesh are laid aside because you are not saying things you already know.
- You are going to speak on what you do not necessarily think about in your mind.
- Every time I speak and teach, I say things by the Holy Spirit I have never thought of before. The insight that the Spirit will give you to speak will sometimes be profound.

When Paul spoke to the Corinthians, what part of them was he speaking to, and from where was he speaking?

____

____

____

____

TRUSTING IN HIS POWER

❖ **<u>1 Corinthians 2:5 NLT:</u>**

I did this so you would trust not in human wisdom but in the power of God.

- That is the summation of prophecy.
- Your faith cannot rest on human wisdom. It can only rest on the power of God.
- It is why religion is called dead and why the Pharisees were dead.

- It is why many religious organizations today start out right, but they lose the power. They are relying on human wisdom.
- They have a form of Godliness, but they deny the power thereof (2 Timothy 3:5).
- Trust only in the power of God.

DISCUSSION:

I can always tell if people are religious or not or if an organization is religious. Are they appealing to the mind and flesh or the Spirit of God? They may say a lot of good things, but there is no power because they are not relying on the resurrection power of God.

Where does your faith rest, and how are you able to maintain His power?

____

____

____

____

SPEAKING FROM WISDOM

❖ **1 Corinthians 2:6 NLT:**

Yet when I am among mature believers, I do speak with words of wisdom, but not the kind of wisdom that belongs to this world or to the rulers of this world, who are soon forgotten.

- Paul is saying in this verse that when we speak wisdom, we speak it to those who are spiritually mature.
- A person who is not born again will not understand spiritual things. They have no way of receiving from you.
- Paul spoke from the wisdom of the Spirit, and he was speaking to spiritually mature people who could receive it.
- Believers have a teachable heart, and they can receive and gain a greater understanding from that revelation that is higher.
- Prophecy will take you to a higher level.

Why can Paul only speak this wisdom to the spiritually mature?

____

____

____

____

DISCUSSION:

When I am in the middle of teaching, sometimes I will stop and prophesy because there is a point where you need to break through to another level. I will share something from the Spirit of God on another level through the Spirit of prophecy. The greater understanding that comes from the Spirit is what judges the present world.

❖ The demonic spirits are aware, and the devil knows certain things he does not want you to know.

- These spirits know things about you that you are not aware they know. They know things about God, and they know that you do not know them.
- If you are aware and confront evil spirits, then they know they have been found out.
- Many religions and denominations are powerless because they do not reveal the position and power of the body of Christ.
- When they do not speak from the power, they are ineffective.
- There is a wisdom that will take you further in the present age that we live, but you need to be able to prophesy from that level and from the other realm. If you do not, you will not be effective.
- We are so far behind in the curve of revelation that God is going to usher in a new move of the prophetic, and it will be through the teens.

❖ The rulers need to be judged, and you judge them by speaking the truth. They know they have come to nothing, but they do not think you know.

- When you, as the body of Christ, start prophesying and proclaiming, they are judged, and they know they are done.

- It is like when a person is found out, who has been hiding it and lying, and you confront them because you know exactly what is going on.
- There is bewilderment within that person on being found out.
- That is what is happening to the enemy through the prophetic.
- It is revealing what is really going on, and the enemies of the body of Christ are getting found out.

Why do you need to speak effectively and from truth?

____

____

____

____

THE UNVEILED MYSTERY

❖ **1 Corinthians 2:7 NLT:**

No, the wisdom we speak of is the mystery of God—his plan that was previously hidden, even though he made it for our ultimate glory before the world began.

- God already had all this established, and He had hidden it, but now He has unveiled it.
- Now we are speaking the mysterious wisdom of God.

- We are speaking the secret wisdom, which is out in the open now.
- Paul said it was once hidden, but now we have been predestined to have it lifting us into God's glorious presence at this time.
- All of this happened before the world began, but it is taking place right now.
- You are chosen at this time to know this and proclaim it.
- That is why you need to let the Spirit prophesy through you.
- Let us receive words to speak forth and proclaim and prophesy over people.
- It is not just about praying for people—it is prophesying over them. We are supposed to damage the enemy.
- Most churches are ineffective because they do not allow the Spirit of revelation to work, and because of it, the gifts of the Spirit are not working. When that's the case, you can't prophesy.
- If you are not allowing the Spirit to speak, then the enemy can come in closer.
- When people prophesy, evil spirits get pushed back.

Why is it so important to prophesy right now?

____

____

____

____

UNDERSTANDING THE TRUTH

❖ **1 Corinthians 2:8 NLT:**

But the rulers of this world have not understood it; if they had, they would not have crucified our glorious Lord.

- None of the rulers of this age understood or recognized the hidden wisdom, and they ended up crucifying Jesus.
- They did not understand the truth, and they fell into a trap.
- God, in His foreknowledge, allowed all of this to happen, yet God never intended for man to fall.
- He allowed it to happen because of free will.
- When you prophesy, you are going to speak the truth, but there is always free will, and people can do what they want with it.
- You must take the prophecies spoken over you and mix them with faith.
- You have to wage war with your prophecy, as Paul told Timothy (1 Timothy 1:18).
- That is how your prophecy comes to pass. You do not just let your prophecy lay there and think it will come to pass.
- We are in a war down here, so we have to wage war with the prophecies that we have received.

What are you to do with the prophecies spoken over you?

____

____

____

____

Why did the people fall into a trap, and why did God allow it to happen?

____

____

____

____

BY HIS SPIRIT WE WILL KNOW

❖ **<u>1 Corinthians 2:9-10 NLT:</u>**

That is what the Scriptures mean when they say, "No eye has seen, no ear has heard, and no mind has imagined what God has prepared for those who love him." But it was to us that God revealed these things by his Spirit. For his Spirit searches out everything and shows us God's deep secrets.

- There is no way you could be where you are in life if you had an anything-goes mentality.

- You cannot have the mentality that whatever God wants will happen; if He does not want it, then it will not be.
- You have to wage war and seek things out in life, or they will not happen.
- We tend to read verse nine and stop there, but if you read verse ten, you will see that God has revealed it to us by His Spirit.

How do the deep secrets of God get to be revealed, and how do things happen in life?

____

____

____

____

❖ I do not know how I would have made it if it were not for the Spirit of God showing me the things He has given me.

- God has prepared it and revealed it all for us by His Spirit.
- They are the deep and hidden mysteries.
- God had a plan that He wanted to reveal, and He revealed it through Paul, and there are things we still do not know.

- When you prophesy, words and wisdom will come out of your mouth that reveal that there is more. These things can be known.
- Begin to recognize the benefits He has bestowed upon you and realize that God has revealed these things to you by the Spirit.
- The Spirit searches out everything, including the deep secrets of God, and He is unveiling them to you.
- The Greek definition says that God has unveiled and revealed these things to us, so they are no longer hidden.
- Churches that are powerless, and do not yield to the Spirit or prophesy, never include Verse 10.
- I used to think that God operated in mysterious ways and that we cannot know or understand them, but that is the complete opposite of what Paul said.
- It is through the Holy Spirit that we can know.

Now that we have access to God's mysteries and hidden secrets, what should you do with them?

____

____

____

____

THE SPIRIT SEARCHES AND REVEALS

DISCUSSION:

If we do not emphasize the power of God and His Spirit in our church services and ministries, then there is no way we can know the deep things. Greek defines it as: "These deep things are searched out by the Spirit diligently." It is the idea of sounding, as in sonar or radar. It sends a signal and waits for a return, and it is always probing and testing. When referencing the depths of God, it's like measuring or using sounding equipment to find out what's out there. It is all wrapped up in the divine counsel of God. The divine counsels and things far beyond human understanding can be revealed by the Spirit. These are the deep counsels of God. It is mentioned in the original Greek language that we can know the deep secrets of God, and it is done by the Spirit searching and then revealing it to us.

THE SPIRIT KNOWS THE THOUGHTS

❖ **1 Corinthians 2:11 NLT:**

No one can know a person's thoughts except that person's own spirit, and no one can know God's thoughts except God's own Spirit.

- The reason Paul says this is to show the different parts of God and the different parts of man.

- In 1 Thessalonians 5:23, Paul mentions the three parts of man: spirit, soul, and body.
- The spirit, soul, and body are three different words, and they all mean different things.
- The soul also has three parts: the mind, will, and emotions.
- The soul is the psychological part of us where we get the word *psyche*—the Greek word for soul.
- You have a spirit, soul, and body.
- You think thoughts, but no one can hear them from the outside unless you verbalize them.
- Paul is saying that your spirit inside of you can hear your thoughts, even though it is a different entity. Your spirit can hear your soul talking.
- It is the same with God; the Spirit of God knows the thoughts of God.

Explain how your spirit knows your thoughts.

____

____

____

____

❖ When you are inquiring of the Lord, you are not inquiring in your mind. You are inquiring in your spirit.

- God will talk to you in your heart. He is not going to talk to you in your mind. God is a Spirit.
- Those who worship God must worship Him in Spirit and in truth, and they are the same thing (John 4:24).
- When God speaks to you, He will not speak to you through your mind or through your body. He will speak to you Spirit to spirit.
- No one can know the thoughts of God except the Spirit of God.
- You cannot know someone else's thoughts because you are not inside them, but their spirit can hear their thoughts in their mind.
- The Holy Spirit can know God's thoughts and communicate with us from God's thoughts, and He will tell us in our hearts.
- We cannot know the motives or intentions of another person because only they know that. However, the Spirit wants to reveal God's thoughts, intentions, and motives to us.

How does the Father communicate with you?

____

____

____

____

HIS KNOWLEDGE IS FREELY GIVEN

❖ **1 Corinthians 2:12 NLT:**

And we have received God's Spirit (not the world's spirit), so we can know the wonderful things God has freely given us.

- Paul is saying that the Spirit of the Lord, which we have received, is not the world's spirit but the Spirit of God.
- We can know the wonderful things that God has given to us.
- We have received the Holy Spirit, not the world's spirit.
- The Holy Spirit will give us the understanding of God's thoughts.
- We will know all the wonderful thoughts God has toward us and the things He has freely given us because He will let us know.
- He will give us all that information, telling it to us in our spirit.
- God is not going to talk to you in your mind.
- He will give you spiritual insight, even through images, but it will come in the Spirit.
- You may think things in your mind because they are interconnected, but they will originate in the Spirit.
- As you mature and grow in the Lord, you will discern between your soul and your spirit.
- It is important that you bring the Word of God and the Spirit of God into it because that is the only thing that can divide between your soul and your spirit.

How do we understand God's thoughts?

____

____

____

____

SPEAKING BY THE SPIRIT

❖ **1 Corinthians 2:13 NLT:**

When we tell you these things, we do not use words that come from human wisdom. Instead, we speak words given to us by the Spirit, using the Spirit's words to explain spiritual truths.

- The Spirit forms the words, then they are given to you, and the understanding comes with it.
- It is done by combining and interpreting spiritual thoughts and spiritual words.
- The Holy Spirit is guiding us.
- God will communicate with you with spiritual words and thoughts, and then He will cause you to speak those forth.
- You will flow from that life and revelation, guided by the Holy Spirit, and you will speak.

- You can have an impression about something, but it is not a thought in your head—it is in your heart.
- Prophecy is speaking the things that the Spirit is teaching you and making them known in this realm through words.

Explain how you prophesy.

____

____

____

____

CHAPTER 5

The Spiritual Ones Understand The Spirit

For those who are led by the Spirit of God
are the children of God.
—Romans 8:14

DISCUSSION:

As you develop the understanding and dynamic of flowing in the Spirit, you will begin to grow on a greater level. People that receive this revelation and flow in the supernatural can get discouraged because they can be shut down. Not everyone around you understands what you do about the supernatural. Some people will resist you because they cannot participate in it for whatever reason. You have to be in a position to understand why and not diminish because others are not flowing in it. When you speak forth by the Spirit and receive revelation, there is a transference or transaction that you are making to other people. Prophecy is revelation that has been verbalized. Sometimes those people are not spiritual, even though they attend church. You can have carnal Christians and unsaved people in the church and friends that claim to be Christians, but they really are not.

Spiritual things have to be interpreted by the Spirit, and a non-spiritual person, who is not partaking in the things of the Spirit has to make a decision when you prophesy to them. They can either humble themselves and receive what the Spirit is saying or resist the Spirit. Many times, spiritual people take rejection the wrong way. They do not understand that you are operating in the truth and in the Spirit. They make decisions not to go with it, and that can include church leaders. That is why you need to have a fellowship of people operating in the Spirit and allowing the Spirit to have His way. A natural man will not receive it.

- ❖ **1 Corinthians 2:14 NLT:**

  But people who aren't spiritual can't receive these truths from God's Spirit. It all sounds foolish to them and they can't understand it, for only those who are spiritual can understand what the Spirit means.

  - People who are not spiritual are not able to receive truths from God's Spirit because God is a Spirit.
  - God is going to transfer spiritual truths only to spiritual people because they can receive them.
  - Only spiritual people can receive from the Spirit.
  - You cannot be a spiritual person if you are not born again.

- You cannot be a spiritual person if you are walking in pride because you're yielding to the flesh and your own understanding.
- Pride entraps you into the soul realm.
- The same thing goes with a religious spirit. It gets you into the mental realm and strictly knowledge, and then there is no experience. Then they restrict you from having an experience or encounter with God, which is a religious spirit.
- I have seen people who used to be spiritual but became carnal and of the mind. They have become religious, and even though they have seen the power of God, they pull back.

Why can't a non-spiritual unbelieving man understand the things of the Spirit?

____

____

____

____

❖ A spiritual person accepts and receives the truth from the Spirit, but to one who is not spiritual, it sounds foolish. They cannot understand it. Only the spiritual can accept and interpret what the Spirit is saying.

- A natural unbelieving man does not accept the things taught by the Spirit. They cannot understand the revelation of the Spirit.

- To an unbelieving man, these things are foolish, absurd, and illogical, as said in Greek.
- It says he is incapable of understanding them because they are spiritually discerned. He does not appreciate them and is unqualified to judge spiritual matters.
- If a person rejects spiritual things, they are unqualified, so they cannot judge you.
- A spiritual person is not subject to this kind of person's judgment because they cannot rightly judge you.

THE SPIRITUAL PERSON CAN JUDGE ALL THINGS

❖ **1 Corinthians 2:15 NLT:**

Those who are spiritual can evaluate all things, but they themselves cannot be evaluated by others.

- A spiritual person is mature and can judge all things in the Spirit because they are spiritually discerning and spiritually mature.
- A spiritual person is able to examine. The original language says they question, examine, and apply what the Holy Spirit reveals.
- However, a spiritual person is not subject to this evaluation, examination, or questioning from an unspiritual person.

- The unbeliever cannot judge you because he cannot understand a person's spiritual nature.

Why can the spiritual person judge?

____

____

____

____

HAVING THE MIND OF CHRIST

❖ **<u>1 Corinthians 2:16 NLT:</u>**

For, “Who can know the Lord’s thoughts? Who knows enough to teach him?” But we understand these things, for we have the mind of Christ.

- Paul is teaching by asking questions.
- He is putting spiritual people at ease by explaining to them that they need to stop allowing themselves to be subject to discouragement from people that do not understand.
- You need to do the same thing.
- You need to allow the purposes of the Lord to be revealed to you and allow Him to instruct you.

- You need to accept the fact that you have the mind of Christ, and you have the understanding.
- You have the faculties to receive from the Spirit of God, and you can be guided by His thoughts and purposes.
- The whole idea in this verse is that we would rely on the Lord to interpret and tell us all that we need to know.
- A spiritual person is going to accept and understand that.
- We cannot allow ourselves to be subject to an unspiritual person's judgment. That is not from the Spirit of God.
- You have to be born again to judge spiritual things.

❖ I never let a person who is either carnal or unsaved judge me or influence me because they are not allowing the Spirit to rule in their lives, nor are they walking in revelation. I do not allow carnal people to have a voice or speak into my life because it could be a hit or miss.

- When you prophesy, you are saying something from the Spirit and saying it out into the air over someone or towards something or someone.
- You can prophesy to mountains to be removed, but you cannot allow someone to judge you. That is not spiritual.

What is the main purpose for having the mind of Christ?

____

____

____

____

MARRIAGE IS A MYSTERY

❖ **Ephesians 5:32 TPT:**

Marriage is the beautiful design of the Almighty, a great mystery of Christ and his church.

- In this verse, we learn of the marriage supper of the Lamb and the bride of Christ.
- Paul said that marriage is a beautiful design.
- It is the mystery of Almighty God about the church.
- The church, the bride, and Jesus are the culmination and sum of everything you will ever prophesy.
- It is all going toward the marriage supper of the Lamb.
- Paul said there is coming a time when tongues and prophecy will cease, and that is when perfection comes (1 Corinthians 13:8).

- When the culmination of the marriage supper of the Lamb happens, there will not be a need for prophecy.
- You will not be prophesying because it will have come to pass.
- Until then, we will speak in tongues and have the gifts of the Spirit because we are being perfected.
- We are not perfected yet.
- As soon as we are made perfect in love, and this comes to an end, there will no longer be a need for prophecy or tongues.

What have we learned about when the marriage supper of the Lamb occurs?

____

____

____

____

PROCLAIMING GODS GRACE

❖ **Colossians 1:3-6 TPT:**

Every time we pray for you our hearts overflow with thanksgiving to Father God, the Father of our Lord Jesus Christ. For we have heard of your devoted lives of faith in Christ Jesus and your tender love toward all his holy believers. Your faith and love rise within you as you access all the treasures of your inheritance stored up in the heavenly realm. For the revelation of the true gospel is as real today as the day you first heard of our glorious hope, now that you have believed in the truth of the gospel. *This is the wonderful message that* is being spread everywhere, powerfully changing hearts throughout the earth, just like it has changed you! Every believer of this good news bears the fruit of eternal life as they experience the reality of God's grace.

- The key is that when you proclaim the gospel and prophesy, it causes people to have the reality of God's grace in their lives.
- It means you will encounter this good news and have the fruit of eternal life, and it is experiential.
- The people you proclaim it to will experience the reality of God's grace.
- It is an encounter and not just head knowledge or hearing the Word. It is being able to experience it.

What does believing in the truth of the gospel do for you and others?

____

____

____

____

PROPHESYING FROM THE RESERVOIR

❖ **Colossians 1:7-9 TPT:**

Our beloved coworker, Epaphras, was there from the beginning to thoroughly teach you the astonishing revelation of the gospel, and he serves you faithfully as Christ's representative. He's informed us of the many wonderful ways love is being demonstrated through your lives by the empowerment of the Holy Spirit. Since we first heard about you, we've kept you always in our prayers that you would receive the perfect knowledge of God's pleasure over your lives, making you reservoirs of every kind of wisdom and spiritual understanding.

- Paul is saying that the Holy Spirit is empowering you, and it is causing love to be demonstrated in wonderful ways.
- There must be a transference of the power of God into something that people see.
- In verse nine, Paul says they have always kept the Colossians in their prayers and that they would receive the perfect knowledge of God's pleasure.
- Your prophetic gift and walking in prophecy, speaking it out, and knowing God's pleasure over your life makes you a reservoir of every kind of wisdom and spiritual understanding.

- God's pleasure over you causes you to store up spiritual understanding and knowledge.
- God takes pleasure in thinking about you and takes pleasure in everything He does. He is not angry like religion has taught you. He is very happy and pleased.
- You constantly feed, letting wisdom and a spiritual understanding of God's pleasure be stored up in you.
- God has made you a reservoir of wisdom and spiritual understanding, and that is how you operate in prophesy.

Explain the idea of being a reservoir as it pertains to prophesy?

____

____

____

____

TRUE RIGHTEOUSNESS LEADS TO FRUITFULNESS AND FULLNESS

❖ **Colossians 1:10 TPT:**

We pray that you would walk in the ways of true righteousness, pleasing God in every good thing you do. Then you'll become fruit-bearing branches, yielding to his life, and maturing in the rich experience of knowing God in his fullness!

- There will be a manifestation of you walking in righteousness.
- That manifestation could be the prophetic utterances that you are speaking.
- You could speak in a prophetic utterance and have no response from people. It may take days, hours, months, or years, but it will bear fruit because you spoke it from the Spirit.
- God is teaching you to be fruit bearers, but He wants you to say it first from the reservoir.
- From these reservoirs, you speak wisdom and understanding from the Spirit.
- You yield to this life and this rich experience of knowing Him and His fullness.

What does walking in true righteousness provide for you and lead you to do?

____

____

____

____

THE REALM OF HIS GLORY

❖ **<u>Colossians 1:11 TPT:</u>**

And we pray that you would be energized with all his explosive power from the realm of his magnificent glory, filling you with great hope.

- You are going to be full and walk in explosive power from this magnificent glory.
- Words are not adequate at times, but prophecy is a way of expressing those things in the best way.
- The Spirit is allowing you to give spiritual words to express in this realm.
- I have seen the glory realm, which is so explosive and full of life and power.
- When I speak words from the Spirit, it still does not completely cover everything you can see from your vantage point.
- For example, when God shows you something, it would take a long time to explain everything.

PROPHESYING HIS GLORIOUS INHERITANCE

❖ **Colossians 1:12-14 TPT:**

Your hearts can soar with joyful gratitude when you think of how God made you worthy to receive the glorious inheritance freely given to us by living in the light. He has rescued us completely from the tyrannical rule of darkness and has translated us into the kingdom realm of his beloved Son. For in the Son all our sins are canceled and we have the release of redemption *through his very blood.*

- We are living in light right now and have a glorious inheritance.
- God rescued us completely from the tyrannical rule of darkness and translated us into the kingdom realm of His beloved son.
- Another reason we need to prophesy is to take the glorious inheritance we have and make people aware of it by stating it.
- The inheritance was freely given to us by living in the light.

What has God rescued us from? What are we translated into?

____

____

____

____

❖ God has rescued us completely from this tyrannical rule of darkness and has translated or taken us across to the other side into the kingdom. The Son has canceled our sins and has released us into redemption.

- Paul is writing about what has already been done.
- These mysteries will be revealed when you meditate on Colossians 1:12-14 and speak from the other realm.
- Prophecy is speaking forth what you have taken from the other realm, which is where the warfare happens.
- You have been translated or transferred out from the spirit of this world and the ruler of darkness and brought into the kingdom of light—into God's kingdom and His throne.
- That is what you should be prophesying; at that point, you are doing warfare.

How does warfare happen?

____

____

____

____

PROPHESYING THE SUPREMACY OF CHRIST

❖ **Colossians 1:15-16 TPT:**

He is the divine portrait, the true likeness of the invisible God, and the firstborn heir of all creation. For in him was created the universe of things, both in the heavenly realm and on the earth, all that is seen and all that is unseen. Every seat of power, realm of government, principality, and authority—it all exists through him and for his purpose!

- Begin to meditate on these verses and prophesy them to whomever you can find that will listen to you.
- Prophesy that God has given us the ability to discern and know the times and seasons and that Jesus Christ is the likeness of the Father, God.
- When you say things like that, all the demons quake.
- Prophesy how everything in the universe was created by Him, and about how every seat of power, every realm of government, principality, and authority all exist because Jesus has formed it.
- That was why Jesus said to Pilate that he had no authority or power against Him unless it had been given by God (John 19:11).
- It is one of the most profound statements one can make.

***When I prophesy, I proclaim the supremacy of Christ and talk about how Jesus Christ is the exact image or portrait of the Divine Father, Our Heavenly Father. He is the likeness of the invisible God.

What should you be prophesying from this verse?

____

____

____

____

How is Christ described in this verse?

____

____

____

____

PROPHESY ABOUT JESUS CHRIST

❖ **Colossians 1:17-18 TPT:**

He existed before anything was made, and now everything finds completion in him. He is the Head of his body, which is the church. And since he is the beginning and the firstborn heir in resurrection, he is the most exalted One, holding first place in everything.

- The most profound thing you can do is to use prophecy as warfare and speak forth the truth to the spirits of darkness.

- Prophesy that God has satisfied everything through Jesus Christ and that He is holding first place, and we are connected with Him through the blood of Jesus.
- Everything in Heaven and earth is brought back to Himself and back to its original intent, restored to innocence again.
- This is the key to your prophetic utterances.
- You must learn to speak what God wants you to say and what He intends, not what is happening.
- He speaks of things that are not as though they were because He wants to bring things back to their original intent (Romans 4:17).

***Begin memorizing verses fifteen through eighteen and continue going over them and getting them in your spirit, so they come out in prophecy. You will begin to speak these things.

What should you be prophesying about from this verse?

____

____

____

____

- What people do not understand about prophecy is that God speaks His intention, even if it is not done.
- God always says His original intent.
- He wants things to be restored back, and that is what Jesus did.
- Everywhere Jesus went, He prayed for people and restored them to the original intent.
- He would raise children to life from the dead, and He would also do this at funerals.
- When people died early, He would raise them from the dead because He was restoring them back to the original intent. God was working through Jesus.

What did Jesus do when He prayed for people?

____

____

____

____

DISCUSSION:

Your healing is just God restoring you back to the original. You will get out of debt and be restored back to your financial security and the original intent. That is what God has for you. You want to begin by prophesying about God helping you in your finances and God helping you in your body. Prophesy about God in your relationships and restoring you back.

❖ When you speak forth, you're bringing correction. You are bringing God's original intent back into this realm and speaking it forth.

- People who hear it can receive it.
- They should always receive the Word of God.
- If they do, they will see it come to pass.
- You must begin by prophesying to your world and then go out and prophesy to others.

What can you prophesy about to see your situation shift?

____

____

____

____

CHAPTER 6

The Spirit Gives Gifts as He Wills

Now, dear brothers and sisters, regarding your question about
the special abilities the Spirit gives us. I don't
want you to misunderstand this.
—1 Corinthians 12:1 NLT

DISCUSSION:

The Spirit gives special abilities and spiritual gifts as He wills. They are also known as endowments and manifestations of the Spirit. These gifts are given to us as graces to express God and His perfect will. When God manifests through one of the gifts of the Spirit, He is bringing correction to a broken world. He is manifesting His will and purpose through the Spirit. Anything you do for the Lord through the gifts of the Spirit, you will have to see as coming from the Heavenly realm, and you are being trusted to portion and deliver it correctly. God does not want us to be ignorant or misinformed. He trusts us to use these gifts wisely and represent His kingdom here on earth.

- **1 Corinthians 12:2 NLT:**

You know that when you were still pagans, you were led astray and swept along in worshiping speechless idols.

- The idols the pagans worshipped had no utterance.
- Prophecy is verbal, but their idols could not speak.
- The speech that we are given is from the living God.
- The Holy Spirit speaks through us, through these endowments, and the giftings inside of us.
- The pagans had no verbal communication with their gods at all.
- Prophecy is speaking forth in a known language through your mouth and lips.
- You speak forth words in a public setting, whether it is to one-on-one or with many people so that others can hear them.
- It is speech-related, and this comes from the Spirit.
- Even though it starts inside you, it ends outside of you through words.

Explain where the utterances we're given come from and how we receive them?

____

____

____

____

SPEAKING BY THE HOLY SPIRIT

❖ **<u>1 Corinthians 12:3 NLT:</u>**

So I want you to know that no one speaking by the Spirit of God will curse Jesus, and no one can say Jesus is Lord, except by the Holy Spirit.

- No one speaking by the Spirit of God will curse Jesus.
- No one can say Jesus is Lord except by the Spirit.
- Paul is laying the groundwork and instilling boundaries.

DISCUSSION:

I can always tell if someone is speaking by a wrong spirit because there will be certain things they will say and certain things they don't say. If somebody speaks and curses Jesus by saying something against the Lord or against the Spirit of God or they have anything against what the Bible says, then we know that is the wrong spirit. Someone who says Jesus is Lord can only say that by the Spirit of God. You want to speak from the power and the influence of the Holy Spirit. You do that by building yourself up by praying in tongues in your belly and by meditating on the Word of God. This builds up the body; individuals, and the corporate body as well

❖ God's long-term plan and strategy is for us to speak from the power and influence of the Holy Spirit within us, and we will not say anything that is contrary. We are also going to judge prophecy as well.

- Paul is talking to people who are sitting there, listening and judging.
- Paul is saying that there are certain things you will not hear in a church service from the Spirit of God, and there are things you will hear from the Spirit of God.
- You have to judge them to tell which spirit it is coming from, and it is very important that you do this.

How do you know if you are speaking by the Holy Spirit?

____

____

____

____

THE SAME SPIRIT

❖ **1 Corinthians 12:4 NLT:**

There are different kinds of spiritual gifts, but the same Spirit is the source of them all.

- The Holy Spirit gives out nine different spiritual gifts.
- There are also impartations, giftings, offices, and endowments.
- The spiritual gifts are distinct and special abilities that have extraordinary power behind them.
- They will not be foolish and powerless, and it will be obvious that they are coming from the Spirit.
- The Spirit grants these things to individuals and empowers them. He gives severally as He wills.
- There will be gifts that you have that other people do not have.
- Not everyone has the gift of prophecy, but everyone can prophesy. There is the gift of prophecy, and it is an endowment from the Spirit.
- There is also the ability to proclaim the Word of the Lord as a believer.
- You can speak forth by the Spirit and pray in the Spirit.
- You can pray in your understanding.
- You can learn to pray in tongues and interpret as well.
- The interpretation of tongues can also be prophecy. When you speak in tongues and interpret them, that is the equivalent of prophecy.
- Whenever I pray, I can speak in English from my Spirit. I don't have to just pray in tongues. I can speak in English and say powerful things by the Spirit, and that is called prophecy.

What abilities as a believer do you have in the Spirit to do the work of the Lord?

____

____

____

____

THE SAME GOD

❖ **1 Corinthians 12:4-5 NLT:**

There are different kinds of spiritual gifts, but the same Spirit is the source of them all. There are different kinds of service, but we serve the same Lord.

- Paul is saying there are a variety of ministries and different ways we can serve, but it is the same Lord that is head over all of them.
- He is head over all the gifts of the Spirit.
- He is in charge and sets these things in individuals as He wills.

❖ **1 Corinthians 12:6 NLT:**

God works in different ways, but it is the same God who does the work in all of us.

- If God is dealing with a person in a certain way, it might not be how He deals with you.
- There are certain distinct ways that He works.
- He accomplishes things according to His will.
- The same God that produces all things, but individually might use a different way.
- Sometimes believers are energized and empowered to do certain things, but they are going to follow in the nine gifts of the Spirit

❖ God may use us in various giftings that He chooses and in a certain way. He may operate through us in the administration gifts, the gift of helps, word of knowledge, word of wisdom, and gifts of healing to accomplish what He wants to do.

- He may not do things in the exact same way every time.
- Sometimes Jesus spit and made mud and put it on people's eyes (John 9:6-11). Other times He cast out a devil (John 9:6).
- Other times He spoke a Word, and people were healed or delivered.
- He did not use the same mode every time.
- Sometimes He said, "Go show yourself to the priest, and you will be healed on the way" (Luke 17:14).

- Jesus used the mode of operation that He did in each situation because He was being led by the Spirit of God.
- He is the same Lord and the same Spirit; that is how we keep in unity.
- You can always sense when it is God operating through a person because it will align with His Word.

In what distinct ways does God work to accomplish His will?

____

____

____

____

DISCUSSION:

When praying for people, I might not put mud on people's eyes, but I use prayer cloths that I pray over and hand out. The faith I have for people to be healed when they take the prayer cloth would be the same faith I have if I were to lay hands on them. It is the same anointing, and I do not doubt they will be healed. I know that each of the prayer cloths we have passed out is effective, but it is not the prayer cloth that heals—it is the anointing. The prayer cloth is just a point of contact. You will have your way of doing things, and God will show you how to be in His perfect will to operate in those gifts.

In prophecy, I often get a vision or a flash and see something, then speak that out. Sometimes I feel heat on my hands; I know it is a healing anointing, and someone will get healed. There are other times I can hear demons screaming, and I know that other people do not hear it, but I know that there are people who are about to get delivered. Prophecy, for me, is more visual, and I speak from what I see, and I do not know word for word what I am going to say. It is how God deals with me specifically. I see things, and then I voice them out.

How have you witnessed Jesus's healing or deliverance in your life?

____

____

____

____

THE SPIRITUAL GIFTS

❖ **<u>1 Corinthians 12:7 NLT:</u>**

A spiritual gift is given to each of us so that we can help each other.

- God has His plan for His Church and His body.
- The Spirit of God is building up the body and encouraging us.
- Each of us has been given a manifestation of the Spirit.
- The Spirit gives us illumination and enables each of us to operate in this certain area.

- It is for the common good and the building up of the body.
- When you prophesy, you are doing it because God wants to help people and build us up into unity.
- That is how He has chosen to do it. It is a gift of the Spirit.

What is the purpose of being given spiritual gifts?

____

____

____

____

WISDOM AND KNOWLEDGE

❖ **1 Corinthians 12:8 AMP:**

To one is given through the [Holy] Spirit [the power to speak] the message of wisdom, and to another [the power to express] the word of knowledge *and* understanding according to the same Spirit;

- The word of wisdom and the word of knowledge are two different gifts of the Spirit.
- The Holy Spirit wants to manifest through one person the power to speak a word of wisdom.
- Wisdom is giving you understanding about the "how-to" in a situation, and it has to do with counseling within a specific thing.

- Knowledge is when you are revealing the situation.
- You can have a word of knowledge about something, but then a word of wisdom is given to you for understanding to cause the right path to be executed in the situation.

What is the difference between a word of wisdom and a word of knowledge?

____

____

____

____

WONDER WORKING FAITH AND GIFTS OF HEALING

❖ **1 Corinthians 12:9 AMP:**

To another [wonder-working] faith [is given] by the same [Holy] Spirit, and to another the [extraordinary] gifts of healings by the one Spirit;

- When you prophesy, you can receive the gift of special faith.
- A boldness comes upon you, and you have no doubt whatsoever that you are hearing from God and speaking from God. It is part of the gift of prophecy.
- When you prophesy, you have to ask God through the Spirit to give you an endowment of special faith.

- Special faith will help you to prophesy as well.
- As the Spirit wills, He will begin to manifest through you.
- The Holy Spirit also gives extraordinary gifts of healing.
- Certain people with the gift of healing will see specific diseases being healed.
- For example, they may have a special gift to see cancer healed. There are others that have a specific gift for healing blood pressure.
- When you are prophesying, you might receive a word of knowledge as well and operate in that gifting simultaneously.
- God may lead you in other giftings when you stand up and prophesy.
- The Lord is directing your speech to where you are going.
- The word goes out into the crowd publicly, but individuals pick up on it and know that the Spirit is talking to them.

***I've had special faith, or the gift of faith comes into me where I could not doubt. Anything that I asked for, I would receive. I would pray for people and see them healed and delivered—there was no doubt at all. It was a special endowment. With special faith, you have no fear.

What are the characteristics of the gift of special faith and the gift of healing?

____

____

____

____

How might God have you operate in other giftings while you are prophesying or moving in a particular gifting?

____

____

____

____

MINISTRY OF THE SPIRIT

❖ **1 Corinthians 12:10 AMP:**

and to another the working of miracles, and to another prophecy [foretelling the future, speaking a new message from God to the people], and to another discernment of spirits [the ability to distinguish sound, godly doctrine from the deceptive doctrine of man-made religions and cults], to another *various* kinds of [unknown] tongues, and to another interpretation of tongues.

- There is the working of miracles, and prophecy, which is speaking forth a message from God to the people.
- Then there is the discerning of spirits, and one who has various kinds of tongues, or diverse tongues.

- I have had the gift of diverse tongues operate in my life where I spoke in different languages with the interpretation of tongues. People tend to get hung up on this because they think that praying in tongues is really the same as speaking in tongues in a public assembly, but it is not the same.

    - Chapter 12 talks about the ministry of the Spirit in a public setting among people in the congregation.
    - When we speak in tongues in the form of a message, there will always be someone there to interpret it.
    - When someone interprets the message, they translate it into the known language from the unknown language or tongue.
    - Nobody knows what the person said in tongues, but someone will say, "I have the interpretation." Then they will stand up and give the interpretation.

- If someone stands up and prophesies by the Spirit, it will be in their known language, which would be the equivalent of tongues and the interpretation of tongues.
- These are all gifts of the Spirit in a public setting.
- In a private setting, you can pray freely in tongues.
- Paul prayed in tongues more than anyone, but in a public setting, he would rather you say something intelligent in their known language.
- Paul said it is better for you to prophesy in a public setting than to speak in tongues.

How does the ministry of the Spirit differ from praying in tongues and speaking in tongues?

____

____

____

____

❖ When the Holy Spirit fell on the people in the Book of Acts, they began to speak in tongues (Acts 2). They were not being told to speak in tongues. It was not a public congregation or assembly where someone got up and gave a message in tongues, and then someone else stood up and interpreted it.

- In the Book of Acts, it was the initial evidence of the baptism of the Holy Spirit when He came upon a group of people that did not know or understand any of this.
- One group was asked if they had received the Holy Spirit, and they said, "We didn't know that there was a Holy Spirit to receive."
- The Holy Spirit came upon them, and they began to speak in tongues, but they were not told this would happen.
- When the Holy Spirit was outpoured on them in the book of Acts, the initial evidence was speaking in tongues because the Holy Spirit had baptized them.
- When Paul or even Jude is talking about praying in the Spirit, it refers to your personal prayer language, or your personal endowment from Heaven.

What is the initial evidence of the Baptism of the Holy Spirit?

____

____

____

____

- When we get Baptized in the Holy Spirit, we begin to speak in tongues and have what we call a prayer language.

  - Your prayer language is not public. It is private.
  - If there is someone to interpret your tongues, then you can speak it out publicly, and the person can interpret it.
  - If there is no interpreter present, you cannot speak in tongues publicly without interpreting because everyone there would not know what you are saying.
  - In a setting where everyone agrees to pray in the Spirit together corporately as believers, that is different because we are not looking for the interpretation. We are looking for everyone to pray in tongues together.
  - If everybody agrees, we pray in tongues and do not have to interpret that.
  - The ministry of the Holy Spirit in a public setting is when someone gets up, gives a message in tongues or prophesies, and operates in the gift of healing or the gift of faith or discerning of spirits. These are public ministries to the body.
  - When you are working with the Holy Spirit, and God gives you a tongue, He knows there must be someone there to interpret that tongue.

- If you give a message in tongues in a public setting, there should be someone there to interpret; if not, you should pray that you receive the interpretation.
- Paul said that when you pray in an unknown tongue, you are not talking to men, you are talking to God, and no one understands you. Your mind does not understand and comprehend it either. That is different than what we are talking about here.

When is it appropriate to give a message in tongues in a corporate setting? When is it okay to pray in tongues in a congregation?

____

____

____

____

DISCUSSION:

When I first met my wife, she would always have a tongue, and I would have the interpretation of the tongues that she was saying. I remember telling her that she should pray that God gives her the interpretation. Now when she prays and speaks forth by the Spirit in tongues in a public setting, she can interpret it and say what the Spirit is saying. All I did was encourage my wife to pray that the Spirit would give her the gift to interpret, and He did. Now she can do both. She can say it in tongues and interpret it. She can pray in tongues, and I can pray in tongues, and we do not have to interpret that.

- Pray that God will give you the gift of interpreting tongues because He will do that.
    - Paul said we should pray that we can interpret it.
    - He said it is better to prophesy in your known language in a public setting.

Why might we want to pray for the interpretation of tongues?

____

____

____

____

- **<u>1 Corinthians 12:11 NLT:</u>**

  It is the one and only Spirit who distributes all these gifts. He alone decides which gift each person should have.

    - There is no wording here that says that we get to choose.
    - Paul says we should ask for the better gifts.
    - It is the Spirit who distributes these gifts.
    - The achievements and abilities are brought by the one and only Holy Spirit.
    - Distributing these gifts to everyone is predetermined in our books and given individually as the Spirit chooses.

How do people receive their giftings?

____

____

____

____

THE BODY OF THE LORD

❖ **1 Corinthians 12:12 NLT:**

The human body has many parts, but the many parts make up one whole body. So it is with the body of Christ.

- The plans and the purposes for why we prophesy and operate in the gifts of Spirit are because each part makes up the whole body.
- We have the word of knowledge and the word of wisdom because we are part of the body of Christ, and we are to edify one another.
- We are in a broken world, but we are all part of Jesus' body on the earth.
- Jesus is the head, and we are the body, and we need to operate in the Spirit and minister to each other.
- Everyone should be praying.

- Whatever gifting you have, you should pray that you can manifest and operate in those giftings because we all need to have a word from God.
- We all need to be healed and delivered.
- We all need to discern and have the discerning of the spirits in our meetings.

Why is each part of the body of believers a vital component in making it thrive?

____

____

____

____

What can you contribute to the body to edify it and see God manifest in power?

____

____

____

____

CHAPTER 7

Building Up the Body Into Unity

Their responsibility is to equip God's people to do his work and build up the church, the body of Christ. This will continue until we all come to such unity in our faith and knowledge of God's Son that we will be mature in the Lord, measuring up to the full and complete standard of Christ.
—Ephesians 4:12-13 NLT

DISCUSSION:

The body of Christ is on the earth through the church, and believers in Jesus Christ form this body. Our main purpose is to build each other up into maturity and have unity in the faith. The only way that we can do this is by the Holy Spirit. The Spirit within each of us wants to express Himself through giftings and powerful endowments of the Spirit that have been given to us. Each person is valuable, and we need each other, and all of these parts form the body of Jesus Christ on the earth. Jesus is still on the earth through us. He is the head, but we are His body.

❖ **1 Corinthians 12:13 NLT:**

Some of us are Jews, some are Gentiles, some are slaves, and some are free. But we have all been baptized into one body by one Spirit, and we all share the same Spirit.

- No matter what people say, there is no difference between us if we are all connected in the Spirit. We are one body.
- The Holy Spirit has baptized us into Himself.
- We have been spiritually transformed so that we are unified together. We are no longer slaves. We are free.
- You could be a slave in the flesh, but whether we are slave or free, Jew or Gentile, we are all baptized or made to drink of the same Spirit.
- The Spirit fills each of us, and we become common amongst each other.
- No matter what status we have in this life, we are all united.
- The gifts of the Spirit, especially prophecy, when spoken in a public setting, build everyone up.
- They are all hearing the same thing together.
- When you speak by the Spirit, it will be very powerful in unifying and building up that group of people.

What has being baptized done for us?

____

____

____

____

EACH PART IS SIGNIFICANT

- **1 Corinthians 12:14 NLT:**

  Yes, the body has many different parts, not just one part.

DISCUSSION:

The body has many parts. We have limbs, organs, and different parts of the body, and we need all those parts. Even if some seem insignificant, we need them. Some people might not have the gift of faith, but they have the discerning of spirits. We might think these are the greater gifts, but where does it say that the apostle is the greatest? Where does it say that the pastor is the least? It doesn't, except for the order in which they are mentioned, but you can find them in other Scriptures where Paul lists them in a different order. I do not believe there is a priority, and I tend to think they are all serving the body. The Apostle Paul did not consider himself to be anyone special. He considered himself to be a servant, and he was an apostle. Paul was one of the major apostles at the foundation, right after Jesus ascended on high. He was one of the bigwigs, yet he considered himself a servant.

❖ **1 Corinthians 12:15 NLT:**

If the foot says, "I am not a part of the body because I am not a hand," that does not make it any less a part of the body.

- Prophecy is a greater gift because you are building up the whole body.
- You can pray for people individually, but prophecy in a corporate setting is very powerful.
- According to Paul, we should all desire to prophesy because it builds up the whole body.
- The foot and the hand are used as an example of comparing the gifts as if one gift is greater or more important than another.
- They are not more important.
- We need one another and each of our giftings.
- The ear does not say, "I'm not important because I'm not an eye."
- Paul continues on to show the idea that we all are important.
- We need to have two eyes and two ears.
- To form a body, you need to have two arms, and you need organs and body parts. We are all arranged to make us one body.

How does each part of the body make up the whole body? Why is Paul more concerned with being a servant?

____

____

____

____

THE FIVE-FOLD MINISTRY AND GIFTS

- **1 Corinthians 12:28 NLT:**

  Here are some of the parts God has appointed for the church: first are apostles, second are prophets, third are teachers, then those who do miracles, those who have the gift of healing, those who can help others, those who have the gift of leadership, those who speak in unknown languages.

DISCUSSION:

In Ephesians four, Paul talks about the five-fold ministry of the church, and he lists them not in the same order as here in Corinthians. They are the apostle, prophet, pastor, teacher, and evangelist. Here he includes a bigger list of the parts in the body that are appointed for the church. He begins with the apostles, prophets, and teachers and then mentions the gifts of the Spirit, the working of miracles, and the gift of healing. Then he mentions the gift of helps; those who serve others, then the gift of administration, where God gives and appoints people to administrate and hold the gift of leadership. Then on the list is the gift of speaking in unknown languages. When he lists this one, he is not talking about people who can speak in tongues versus those who cannot; he is talking about publicly giving a message in tongues. It is those who can speak in an unknown tongue publicly as a gift and impartation of the Spirit. He is not referring to those who have received the baptism of the Holy Spirit and speak in tongues, nor is he talking about our personal prayer language when we speak in tongues. Paul here is mixing and matching the gifts of the Spirit, whereas, in Ephesians, he talks specifically about the five-fold. There are also the fruits of the Spirit. They are the manifest personality of God. The fruits influence people and cause them to act a certain way, but they are not the same as the gifts. When Paul lists the apostle, prophet, teachers, and gifts of healing and miracles, it shows that different portions are being given out and that they all must manifest in a service. In a service, how many times do any of these gifts manifest?

- ❖ The gifts of the Spirit should be manifesting within the service, where God is manifesting.

    - Are people who speak in tongues in a public setting interpreting the tongues? Do they have the gifts of healing, and are they apostles, pastors, or teachers? The answer is no.

- When each person is given their assignment, and they are operating in it, then together we fulfill the body of Christ.
- We should strive earnestly for these gifts and the greater gifts.
- We're to acquire the goal and be built up in a more excellent way.
- These graces that God has predetermined for us will be even greater gifts, and He wants us to excel in the greater gifts.
- The greater gift is that you should desire to prophesy.
- The Lord wants us to exercise our vocal gifts and speak forth through us to build people up, not tear them down.

Why is it significant that we operate in our giftings and prophesy?

____

____

____

____

LOVE IS YOUR HIGHEST GOAL

❖ **1 Corinthians 14:1 NLT:**

Let love be your highest goal! But you should also desire the special abilities the Spirit gives—especially the ability to prophesy.

THE AMPLIFIED TRANSLATION:

❖ **1 Corinthians 14:1 AMP:**

Pursue [this] love [with eagerness, make it your goal], yet earnestly desire *and* cultivate the spiritual *gifts* [to be used by believers for the benefit of the church], but especially that you may prophesy [to foretell the future, to speak a new message from God to the people].

- Love should be your motivation for doing everything.
- Paul is saying that we should make it our goal to desire and cultivate the spiritual gifts.
- The spiritual gifts are to be used by believers for the benefit of the church.
- Paul puts emphasis on the gift of prophecy as the most important gift.
- He talks about this gift more than all the others.
- Chapter 14 is mostly dedicated to this very one gift.
- It is so that we would speak the message of God to the people.
- Prophecy can be futuristic and forth-telling, not just foretelling. It is speaking forth the will of God.
- You are also not responsible for making it happen. You are responsible for speaking it out.
- God then mixes that with the faith of the people.

Why is love your motivation for everything? How is it that love is to coincide with operating in the gifts?

___

___

___

___

- ❖ Paul told Timothy that he should wage war with the prophecies he was given. (1 Timothy 1:8).

    - Paul taught him to use his prophecies in prayer and warfare as weapons against the enemy.
    - We are to speak forth and enforce the prophetic words we have received. Prophecy is so important, especially in the coming days, so we need to speak forth God's will over our lives and the lives of others.
    - Inform others to take the prophetic words they have received and wage war with them.

Why is prophecy of such significance, and what is it doing for people?

___

___

___

___

THE SPIRIT SPEAKS MYSTERIES THROUGH PROPHECY

❖ **1 Corinthians 14:2 AMP:**

For one who speaks in an *unknown* tongue does not speak to people but to God; for no one understands him *or* catches his meaning, but by the Spirit he speaks mysteries [secret truths, hidden things].

- We can pray in tongues and speak publicly in tongues, but to speak publicly, you will need to have an interpreter.
- The interpretation enables the people hearing it to understand what you are saying. Otherwise, it is not worth anything to the ones hearing it.
- In a corporate setting, we as believers can agree to pray in tongues together. When we pray as a congregation out loud, we do not need to have an interpreter.
- When you operate as part of the service with tongues, interpretation, and prophecy, you must operate decently and with order.
- If you give a message in tongues, you will have to interpret your message or else do not give it.
- If there is no one present to interpret your message, then you should pray that you can prophesy or speak it out in the known language.

When is it ok to speak in tongues in a public setting?

____

____

____

____

PROPHECY STRENGTHENS OTHERS

❖ **1 Corinthians 14:3 NLT:**

But one who prophesies strengthens others, encourages them, and comforts them.

- If you can speak in tongues and know what you are saying, then you can interpret your tongues and do both.
- You can pray and say something in the Spirit publicly to the congregation, and the Spirit will give you the translation or interpretation.
- When you speak in tongues and have the interpretation, and then speak that out, that is equivalent to prophesy.
- If there is no one there with the gift of interpretation, then someone will speak in tongues, and there will not be an interpretation. No one will know what was said.

- Paul is trying to prevent these things from happening.
- If there is no one to interpret, do not speak in tongues.
- Paul knew that the people knew what their giftings were, and they knew each other.
- They knew if a certain person was there and whether they had the gift of interpretation of tongues or if someone had a tongue to give out.
- It would be better if you prayed and asked God to give you the gift of prophecy so that you would not need an interpreter in your congregation.
- When you prophesy in your known language, you do not need interpretation.
- That is why Paul is saying this is the best gift to have.
- Paul is telling us to pray that we get this endowment or gifting.
- Of all the giftings, prophecy should be your main prayer request.

How does prophesying in a service stand true as the better option for ministering the gifts of the spirit?

____

____

____

____

DISCUSSION:

In verse three, if you do the word study, it talks about how the one who prophesies speaks to the people for the purpose of edification to build them up, promote their spiritual growth, and speak words of encouragement. There is the building up and the edification that promotes spiritual growth, then there is speaking words of encouragement, and finally, upholding and advising concerning matters of God. There is a council concerning the matters of God, and it is all part of prophecy. If you do the word study, the person who prophesies is speaking consolation to comfort someone compassionately. We are to edify people in their spiritual growth, speak words of encouragement, uphold, advise, and counsel concerning the matters of God. These are all involved in the gift of prophecy.

PROPHECY STRENGTHENS THE CHURCH

❖ **1 Corinthians 14:4-5 NLT:**

A person who speaks in tongues is strengthened personally, but one who speaks a word of prophecy strengthens the entire church. I wish you could all speak in tongues, but even more I wish you could all prophesy. For prophecy is greater than speaking in tongues, unless someone interprets what you are saying so that the whole church will be strengthened.

- Paul is saying that you are really just speaking to yourself and God if there is no interpreter.
- You are edifying yourself through tongues, but prophecy is building up the whole body.
- The one who prophesies edifies the church, promotes their spiritual growth, and brings spiritual wisdom, devotion, holiness, and joy.
- Paul emphasizes that we could all speak in tongues, but even more so that we would prophesy.
- Paul wants the whole church to be strengthened.
- The whole plan of God, the mystery, and the prophetic sequence being revealed is that God, at the end of the age, is bringing us to the unity of the faith and maturity.
- It is so the bride of Christ is without spot or wrinkle, and we are being prepared for the wedding day
- It is coming through the gifts of the Spirit and the administrations of the Spirit.
- It has to do with the governments and administrations that God gives.

Who is strengthened by tongues, and who is strengthened by prophecy? What is the plan of God for strengthening the church?

____

____

____

____

❖ **1 Corinthians 14:6 NLT:**

Dear brothers and sisters, if I should come to you speaking in an unknown language, how would that help you? But if I bring you a revelation or some special knowledge or prophecy or teaching, that will be helpful.

- Believers can speak in tongues, but when in a public setting, it will not benefit you unless someone can interpret the tongues.
- If someone speaks in their known language clearly, whether it is a revelation, word of knowledge, teaching, prophecy, or instruction, you will develop spiritual maturity because there is an understanding.
- It is the same thing when someone plays a musical instrument. They must play the notes clearly, or no one will know the melody.

GOD'S SEQUENTIAL TIMELINE

- **1 Corinthians 14:7 NLT:**

  Even lifeless instruments like the flute or the harp must play the notes clearly, or no one will recognize the melody.

  - There is a sequence, and there is a way to do it for people to understand what is being played.
  - The instruments must be played in order so people can recognize the tune.
  - The person playing the instrument will have to play a certain note at a certain time in a sequence for the melody to be known.
  - These lifeless instruments produce a sound, but they must be played with distinct notes and tones for people to recognize them.
  - It is the same with the gifts of the Spirit—they must be clear and concise.

- If a clarion call is given out, or if someone gives out a war cry through a horn, announcing war, they will blow the shofar, and the soldiers will know it is a call to war.

  - People know what certain sounds mean. There is a purpose for them, and it has to be something that everybody recognizes.

- If you speak intelligible words, everyone will understand what you are saying.
- However, no one knows what is happening if you speak in an unknown tongue. It isn't common, and there is no unity.
- In the Greek translation, when you speak in an unknown tongue, it says that you are wasting your breath or talking into the air.
- When you speak in tongues and pray, you are talking to God and not to men.
- Your mind is not fruitful, but you are praying out the mysteries in the Spirit.
- It is the same thing when God speaks to you in a dream.
- If you do not understand what the dream is really saying, it does not help you.
- You have to be able to understand what your dream means.

Explain why the comparison is made between the instruments playing their certain notes and sequence and people operating in the gifts of the Spirit?

____

____

____

____

DISCUSSION:

It is often very clear to me when I dream because I have developed and structured my heart and mind with the Word of God. At night, my spirit can communicate with my soul, and it will be a clear image. Sometimes your mind does not interpret things correctly, it knows what it has seen and received, but it does not have the proper tools to interpret it. I have noticed over the years that my dreams became clearer as I built myself up in the Word of God. It is the same with tongues and interpretation. We have to focus on speaking words of wisdom and words of knowledge in the known language and speak forth out of the heart of God, in your known language. That is what we call prophecy.

CHAPTER 8

Speaking By The Spirit

And everyone present was filled with the Holy Spirit and began speaking in other languages, as the Holy Spirit gave them this ability.
—Acts 2:4 NLT

DISCUSSION:

Prophecy builds up the believer and the body of Christ. It is spoken in the known language, but it comes from the Spirit of God, and its purpose is to edify the people. Paul emphasizes that prophecy is the gift of the Spirit we should use for all people to understand and receive. We can speak in tongues in an unknown language when we have an interpreter or when we, as the body in a service, all agree to speak in tongues. If someone were to speak out in tongues solely, the congregation might pick up in their spirit that something amazing was said, but they will not know what it is. In order to avoid misunderstandings, it is best to speak in the known language unless someone is available to interpret the tongues.

- **1 Corinthians 14:10 NLT:**

There are many different languages in the world, and every language has meaning.

- Many different languages are being spoken.
- When you speak in the Spirit, God allows you to speak in a known language, but you just don't know what it is.
- Paul mentions in 1 Corinthians 13 about the tongues of angels. There may be an ancient language spoken that is not available today, but you may pick up on pieces of it in your spirit.
- That was what was happening at Babel. The languages were scattered so that no one could talk together (Genesis 11:1-9).
- All the languages came into being and were dispersed at the Tower of Babel to confuse the people.
- Instead of there being one language, they were speaking many other languages.
- That was done because the people in Babel were evil and in agreement with each other.
- God said that whatever they imagined they would be able to do. He had to come down and confuse their languages.
- That was how we got all the different languages in the world.
- God limited man because man in their rebellion would be able to circumvent and be lawless, and He could not have that happen.

Why did God confuse the languages of the people at Babel

____

____

____

____

DISCUSSION:

On the day of Pentecost, when the Spirit of God came, He caused us to be unified in the Spirit by baptizing us in the Spirit (Acts 2:1-13). When we speak in tongues, we speak in these different languages that we do not know as a sign of the Holy Spirit. In a public setting, there is the gifting of the Spirit where all the different languages may be known. That is what happened in Jerusalem when the Holy Spirit was outpoured on the day of Pentecost. People heard their language being spoken, but they knew that the 120 who spoke did not know that language and were not from their country. The multitudes knew that it was a sign from God.

❖ **1 Corinthians 14:11 NLT:**

But if I don't understand a language, I will be a foreigner to someone who speaks it, and the one who speaks it will be a foreigner to me

- When you get baptized in the Holy Spirit, understand that you may speak an ancient language or a language that is known in some part of the world.

- Paul says that when you are in a congregation, foreigners will be there, and they may not understand you if you are speaking in a tongue.

Why is the language and what we speak so significant to prophecy?

____

____

____

____

PROPHECY BUILDS UP THE CHURCH

❖ **1 Corinthians 14:12 NLT:**

And the same is true for you. Since you are so eager to have the special abilities the Spirit gives, seek those that will strengthen the whole church.

- There are manifestations of the Spirit that will excel and build up the church. One of which is the gift of prophecy.
- Anyone who speaks in tongues should pray for the ability to interpret what they have spoken.

- Everyone who gets baptized in the Holy Spirit receives their prayer language. As in the Book of Acts, they spoke in tongues but were not told to do it; it just happened. That is why it was a sign. If you are baptized in the Holy Spirit, the initial evidence is speaking in tongues.

  - Paul prayed in the Spirit more than anyone.
  - Praying in the Spirit *is* being baptized in the Holy Spirit.
  - Everyone has the ability to speak in tongues, but it will be in a different language.
  - Speaking in tongues is the complete reversal of what happened at the Tower of Babel.

What are we to focus on when we are ministering to people?

____

____

____

____

PRAYING FOR INTERPRETATION

- **1 Corinthians 14:13 AMP:**

  Therefore let one who speaks in a tongue pray that he may [be gifted to] translate *or* explain [what he says].

- When you have prayed, and the Lord has given you a message in tongues and the ability to interpret your tongues, it is equivalent to prophesying.
- If you pray to God and ask Him to give you the ability to prophesy, then you are going to speak in your known language so that everyone understands what you are saying.
- That would be the same as tongues and interpretation.

How is prophesying and interpretation of tongues beneficial and essentially the same thing?

____

____

____

____

THE SPIRIT IS PRAYING

❖ **1 Corinthians 14:14 NLT:**

For if I pray in tongues, my spirit is praying, but I don't understand what I am saying.

- Speaking in tongues is not a mental exercise.
- Your spirit prays, but your mind does not participate.

- You do not understand what you are saying, but your spirit is praying it out.
- Even though you hear someone praying in tongues with their voice and you see their lips and tongue moving, their spirit is the one who is praying, even though the body is manifesting.

PRAYING IN THE KNOWN AND UNKNOWN LANGUAGE

❖ **1 Corinthians 14:15 NLT:**

Well then, what shall I do? I will pray in the spirit, and I will also pray in words I understand. I will sing in the spirit, and I will also sing in words I understand.

- There is praying in the Spirit and singing in the Spirit, and there is also praying in the understanding or in your known language. There is also singing in your known language, and you can do any of these.
- The Holy Spirit within you is doing the spiritual things.
- The Holy Spirit gives you a translation or an interpretation to sing it in English or your native language.
- This verse is saying, "I will sing with my spirit, but I will also sing with my mind or my understanding.

What shall we do when we pray in tongues and do not understand what we are saying?

____

____

____

____

SPEAKING SO OTHERS UNDERSTAND

❖ **1 Corinthians 14:16 NLT:**

For if you praise God only in the spirit, how can those who don't understand you praise God along with you? How can they join you in giving thanks when they don't understand what you are saying?

- When you are exercising the gifts of the Spirit, people have to be able to say Amen or give thanks to God for what is being proclaimed.
- If people don't know what you are saying, they cannot do that.
- Stay focused and ask God to give you the giftings to edify the people.

Why is it important that we speak in the known language? In tongues with interpretation?

___

___

___

___

❖ **1 Corinthians 14:17-18, 20 NLT:**

I thank God that I speak in tongues more than any of you. But in a church meeting I would rather speak five understandable words to help others than ten thousand words in an unknown language. Dear brothers and sisters, don't be childish in your understanding of these things. Be innocent as babies when it comes to evil but be mature in understanding matters of this kind.

- Paul says that we are not to be immature like children.
- We can be infants in understanding evil.
- We can be completely innocent and be infants in knowing evil and good.
- Children, and infants, are innocent, so they do not have the ability to discern between good and evil until they get older.

- Paul says, be as infants as far as evil goes, but in your thinking, do not be like a child that is immature. Be an adult.
- Your minds must be mature as adults.
- You have to take this step now, that as far as evil goes, you will be like an infant.
- As far as being mature, you will be like an adult in the way that you think.

Why are we asked to be innocent and mature?

____

____

____

____

❖ **1 Corinthians 14:21 NLT:**

It is written in the Scriptures: "I will speak to my own people through strange languages and through the lips of foreigners. But even then, they will not listen to me," says the Lord.

- The Lord prophesied right here in the Old Testament, and He is talking about tongues.
- Tongues were prophesied, and this outpouring of the Spirit was prophesied.

❖ **1 Corinthians 14:22 NLT:**

So you see that speaking in tongues is a sign, not for believers, but for unbelievers. Prophecy, however, is for the benefit of believers, not unbelievers.

- Paul is talking about a congregation that might have unbelievers present, and that is where prophecy becomes key instead of tongues.
- Unknown tongues are meant as a supernatural sign and are not understood.
- Even when unbelievers do not understand what is happening in the service, and somebody speaks in their native language, they know that this person does not know that language, and it blows them away.
- They knew that the person speaking did not know their language, and they knew it had to have been God speaking to them.

When is prophecy key to use instead of Speaking in tongues?

____

____

____

____

- **1 Corinthians 14:23-24 NLT:**

Even so, if unbelievers or people who don't understand these things come into your church meeting and hear everyone speaking in an unknown language, they will think you are crazy. But if all of you are prophesying, and unbelievers or people who don't understand these things come into your meeting, they will be convicted of sin and judged by what you say.

- I have seen this happen with someone who spoke Arabic. The person was praying in tongues, but God was directly speaking to them. They were crying and telling me what was being said, but I knew this person did not speak Arabic.
- They were just baptized in the Holy Spirit, but it revealed the heart.
- If you are speaking and there is no interpretation, then people think you are crazy, but if you speak by the Spirit and it is a known language to the person, then that is a sign.
- For the believer, when you speak by the Spirit in a meeting, you can operate with tongues, interpretation, and prophecy.
- If unbelievers are there, or some people do not understand this, they will be convicted of sin and judged by what you say.
- If you are prophesying and they can hear what you are saying and reveal their heart, then they are going to repent.

- The only way that tongues would benefit an unbeliever is if they understood the language, which would be a sign that does happen.
- In a believers meeting, we can pray in tongues and interpret or prophesy, and everyone understands what is going on.

❖ When there are people that do not understand the manifestations of the Spirit, Paul advises that you operate in a way where people understand.

- The unbeliever has to be convicted, and to be convicted they cannot sit there and think you are crazy.
- When an unbeliever or outsider comes in, and you prophesy and say something that they know you could not know about them, their hearts are revealed, and they become convicted.
- If you speak in a tongue that was Spirit-led, and they understand that language, that is a sign too, and they will repent.
- The whole idea is that the secrets of their hearts must be laid bare, and then they fall down on their face and worship God, declaring that He is among you.

Why is prophecy most effective in a church service?

____

____

____

____

❖ **1 Corinthians 14:25 NLT:**

As they listen, their secret thoughts will be exposed, and they will fall to their knees and worship God, declaring, "God is truly here among you."

- If we have a meeting where there are unbelievers, then we need to do it decently and in order through prophecy. Then when you prophesy, you are prophesying secrets and mysteries that are in a known language, and the hearers will hear that.
- The power of God will convict people, and if there is an unbeliever there, they can repent.
- If they do not understand the language you are speaking, there is no way for them to repent. Paul is calling them to be in order, and we need to understand this.
- That's why it is better to prophesy and speak in the known language.

TAKING TURNS IN A SERVICE

❖ **<u>1 Corinthians 14:25-31 NLT:</u>**

Well, my brothers and sisters, let's summarize. When you meet together, one will sing, another will teach, another will tell some special revelation God has given, one will speak in tongues, and another will interpret what is said. But everything that is done must strengthen all of you. No more than two or three should speak in tongues. They must speak one at a time, and someone must interpret what they say. But if no one is present who can interpret, they must be silent in your church meeting and speak in tongues to God privately. Let two or three people prophesy, and let the others evaluate what is said. But if someone is prophesying and another person receives a revelation from the Lord, the one who is speaking must stop. In this way, all who prophesy will have a turn to speak, one after the other, so that everyone will learn and be encouraged. Remember that people who prophesy are in control of their spirit and can take turns.

- At the end of this chapter, Paul summarizes everything and says that when they meet, he wants to call some boundaries.
- Today, most churches do not allow the gifts of Spirit to operate, which is wrong.
- Back then, Paul said when we get together, "One has a song they want to sing that the Spirit has given them. One has something

they want to teach. One has a special revelation that God has given them. One wants to speak in tongues, and another wants to interpret."

- He said that we should let everything be done decently in order and all for the purpose of strengthening the people.
- We are to limit it to a certain amount of time where two or three should speak in tongues, one at a time, and someone must come up and interpret what they all said.
- Let each person take their turn, but make sure there is an interpreter. If no one is present to interpret, they must be silent in the church and speak in tongues to God privately.
- If an interpreter is present, you can speak it out publicly and let the person interpret it.
- Let two or three people prophesy. Bring people up, let them prophesy, and let the others evaluate what is being said.
- The rest of us must sit there, pay attention and carefully weigh what is being said.

Why should we have organization in a prophetic service?

____

____

____

____

❖ If someone is prophesying and another person receives a revelation from the Lord, the one who is speaking must eventually yield to another person and stop.

- If people are prophesying and they are taking their turn, you have to be able to yield to another person who is seated and has a revelation.
- They may not have a prophecy; they may have a revelation.
- You have to give way to that person if that gift is valid.
- You need to bring them up and let them share their revelation.
- The first one speaking must yield.
- In other words, do not keep talking past a certain point.
- Prophesy, then yield to the next person who has a revelation.
- If an interpreter is present, you can speak it out publicly and let the person interpret it.
- If you are doing a sequence of tongues and interpretations or a sequence of prophecies, the person should announce, "I have a tongue." Then the person who can interpret the tongues should come up and be ready.
- Then you would call up the one sitting with a revelation and make sure they are in sequence with being able to share in this way, and then all can prophesy.
- It is one by one, and everyone can be instructed and encouraged.

How should a service effectively run, so all people leading have a chance to prophesy or move in their gifting?

____

____

____

____

❖ **1 Corinthians 14:32 NKJV:**

The spirits of the prophets are subject to the prophets.

- That means that a person is actually in control of their spirit, and at a certain point, you need to be still and yield to the next person.
- You cannot just stay up there and take over. You have got to yield so that the Spirit can use other people.
- People say, "I cannot stop speaking." It is not true. You can stop.
- Paul said that prophecy is under the control of the speaker.
- That means you do have control, and you are supposed to yield.
- God is a God of order, not disorder.
- He is going to meet the needs of His people, and He will do that in an orderly fashion, is what Paul is saying.
- God is the source of prophecy, which is what it literally says, and is under the prophet's control.

- At any moment, he needs to be able to yield and let the Spirit use someone else.
- The Word of God did not originate with man. It originated with God Himself.
- The gifts of the Spirit originated with God, not man, and there are certain things that God wants to do, and He dictates how everything is to be done.
- You cannot say this is how we will do it because God gave the gift, to begin with, so we need to stay within the confines of that.

Why must we yield to one another in a service?

____

____

____

____

BE READY TO PROPHESY AT ALL TIMES

❖ **<u>Corinthians 14:37 NASB:</u>**

If anyone thinks that he is a prophet or spiritual, let him recognize that the things which I write to you are the Lord's commandment.

- Paul was saying he received all of this from the Lord.
- If you think you are advanced and a prophet and you are prophesying, then you need to keep within the confines of this verse. These were Paul's last words to the Corinthians.

❖ **1 Corinthians 14:39-40 NLT:**

So, my dear brothers and sisters, be eager to prophesy, and don't forbid speaking in tongues. But be sure that everything is done properly and in order.

- We are to speak in tongues, and no one is supposed to be forbidden from speaking in tongues.
- We are to be eager. That means everyone should desire to speak in tongues and prophesy.
- It should be done properly, in order, and in a decently, orderly manner.
- From the beginning, God wanted us to be built up and joined together, and everything should support that goal in a service.
- We should be meditating on Scripture and the truth about the church, the body, and God's mindset.
- Then you can realize the inheritance you have, the revelation of the Spirit, the hope, and the love you have.

- When you get into these things, you realize the Spirit wants to build people up and mature them.
- The goal here is to do it the right way and always do it.
- In order to do it all the time, you must be ready.
- You have to be prepared.
- No matter where I go, I am always praying that I will get a word so that I am ready if I am called upon. I am asking the Spirit all the time, what should I say? What should I do?

Why must we do things the right way or properly?

____

____

____

____

❖ The Spirit is so faithful. As I pray in tongues and I interpret, He is always faithful to give me a message and give me a word that I can share.

- That is what you need to do. You need to study just one verse every day and get something out of it and ask the Spirit to prepare you.

DISCUSSION:

The way it happened for me was that for many years He prepared for what I am doing now. He would give me a verse and a revelation in the morning, and by the end of the day, I would be sitting with someone, sharing and talking about the verse. Over the years, I developed a way of delivering that message and moving in the Spirit. I would pray in the Spirit and interpret my tongues, then talk to people and give them messages. I did that constantly. It was before I was even officially in the ministry. I encourage you to move in the Spirit now and be ready to share something. Pick any subject you want, start studying the Scriptures for it, and develop your doctrine based on what the Scriptures say. As you do that, you will have words, revelation, and wisdom that you can share. I would find somebody to talk with about it. I would call up a friend and begin talking to them about what God was saying or doing and get a discussion going. The Spirit will use you to relay that information. It becomes the platform for prophesying because after you share these truths, the fountain inside of you will increase, and you will feel the flow. You will feel that power and release it to others.

How do you prepare yourself to share revelation that God is giving you?

____

____

____

____

CHAPTER 9

Love Is The Greatest

If I speak in the tongues of men and of angels, but have not love,
I am a noisy gong or a clanging cymbal.
—1 Corinthians 13:1 ESV

DISCUSSION:

In the last 2,000 years, God has encountered prophecy being revealed through the church. We are seeing it come forth through this generation in the sequence of the prophetic timeline. In the womb, today, are many prophets and prophetesses being born, and the mystery of the prophetic is being revealed. We have seen in 1 Corinthians Chapters 12 and 14 how the gifts of the spirit and prophecy have been used to edify and encourage the body of Christ. In 1 Corinthians 13:13, there is revelation that this three remain; faith, hope, and love. There is the faith that you can operate in the gifts of the Spirit. There is hope where there is exhortation, but the greatest of these is love. You have the fruit of the Spirit and the gifts of the Spirit, but love is the greatest of all. The love chapter is put there in the middle of Chapters 12 and 14 on purpose. Both are talking about the gifts of Spirit. At the end of Chapter 12, Paul talks about the gifts and how they operate, then he says he will show us a better way to operate in those giftings. It is through love. Love is the greatest.

- The whole idea about prophecy and the gift of the Spirit is that it is for other people. You do it in love, and you love people.
- As long as you keep your focus on the Spirit of God and loving people, then you will operate in the ministry of Jesus.
- You will operate in the gifts and do it properly because you are thinking of others.
- If you get into self-exaltation or draw attention to yourself, and your motive for doing it is for yourself, then you will be judged for that.
- It does not benefit people, and you are like a clanging cymbal.
- You could give your body to be burnt for your faith, but if you do not have love, then it is worthless.

Why is love the greatest, and how does it pertain to prophesy?

____

____

____

____

DISCUSSION:

When I pray in the Spirit, and I hear people praying in the Spirit, I can tell if they are praying correctly from deep within their spirit versus if they are up in their soul. I have heard intercessors pray, and the power of God was so strong because they had really developed in praying from the depths. There is a praying in the Spirit that moves mountains, and you do not even know what you are saying, but you can feel that you are praying from the depths. When somebody prophesies, I can tell whether they are prophesying from the depths. There is an intensity there and a lot of power available. Looking further into it, it is because the person is walking in love. That is the connection and the conduit to this amazing power from the depths.

❖ You do not want to operate in the gifts of Spirit on the surface, where you are just functioning. There is a depth, and you can feel this in certain people.

- There is a presence around people where the power of God is so strong because they have connected deep within their hearts in love.
- Paul says, "If I could speak in all the languages of the earth and angels but did not love others, I would be a noisy gong or a clanging cymbal."
- He is mentioning that there are tongues of angels as well as men, and you can pray in tongues, but if you do not have love, you are just making noise.

What is one thing that causes people to have a greater presence of God on them?

____

____

____

____

❖ I have sensed in my spirit that people are not always praying from love, and correction needs to happen. I believe that you will become powerful prophets when you pray, and that you will be powerful in the gifts of the Spirit. I am hopeful that you will operate from the depths of love. It can happen to where God can perfect you in love.

- We do not want to be a clanging symbol when we pray in tongues. We do not want to be annoying.
- One of the translations in Greek says, when you pray in tongues without love from the depths, you are an annoying distraction.
- I know this to be true because I have heard it.
- I have heard people pray in tongues, and it was not from the depths, nor was it in love.
- They were praying in tongues, but if you are not doing it in love to help others grow, then you are just an annoying distraction. That is what the Amplified Version says.

LOVING OTHERS QUALIFIES YOU

❖ **<u>1 Corinthians 13:2 NLT:</u>**

If I had the gift of prophecy, and if I understood all of God's secret plans and possessed all knowledge, and if I had such faith that I could move mountains, but didn't love others, I would be nothing.

- Paul is saying that if you understood God's secret plans and had the gift of prophecy, if you possessed all knowledge, and you had such great faith that you could move mountains, but did not love others, you would be nothing.
- Even if you have understanding of the deep mysteries in the Spirit and possess all this knowledge with mountain-moving faith, you are nothing if you do not love others.
- There is a reason he is saying this, and I saw that in Heaven, Jesus is going to say to people, "I never knew you" (Matthew 7:21-23).
- Why would Jesus say that?
- Those people prophesied in His name, healed the sick, and did all these miracles, but He said, "I never knew you."
- It is because they did not have an intimate relationship with Jesus, and they were not walking in love. This is the truth.

What happens to people who have operated in the gifts and miracles but have not loved?

____

____

____

____

- **1 Corinthians 13:3 NLT:**

  If I gave everything I have to the poor and even sacrificed my body, I could boast about it; but if I didn't love others, I would have gained nothing.

  - Paul is showing people that it is not about going through the motions or actions of ministry.
  - Some ministries operate in power and all the gifts and manifestations of the Spirit, yet you find out they are living in sin and doing terrible things.
  - That can happen because the gifts of the Spirit are still working in each individual to build up the body, but the ones in sin have disqualified themselves.
  - Paul said he could be disqualified if he did not discipline his body. He said, "That after he preached Christ he could be

disqualified," because he was not spirit ruled, he was body ruled. We have to make that decision.

- People can live in sin and still be used of God in the gifts of the Spirit. We want to prophesy from the depths of love.
- There is more of a presence and power when you operate in love towards others.

What disqualifies you?

____

____

____

____

❖ **1 Corinthians 13:4 NLT:**

Love is patient and kind. Love is not jealous or boastful or proud.

- Love stays in there longer and is patient and peaceful.
- There is a patience and a serenity with love.
- Love endures, and love is kind and thoughtful.
- It is not jealous or envious, and it does not brag.
- It is not boastful, proud, or arrogant.

- If you are prideful, it is a characteristic of you as a person, whereas arrogance is more of an outward action.
- You can be prideful and hide it.
- There is even a false pride, but arrogance is when you outwardly manifest it to others. We are not going to be prophesying from these places.
- We are going to be patient and kind, and thoughtful.
- We are not going to be envious, and we are not going to brag.
- We are not going to be proud or arrogant.

How do you love from a genuine place?

____

____

____

____

❖ **<u>1 Corinthians 13:5 NLT:</u>**

...or rude. It does not demand its own way. It is not irritable, and it keeps no record of being wronged.

- When you minister to people through the gifts of the Spirit, you cannot be rude and self-seeking.

- You cannot have an ounce of selfishness in you, or it causes the flow of the Spirit to be hindered, and that is what Paul is talking about here.
- If you are rude, you cannot be kind.
- If you are self-seeking, you cannot be an outflow to others or have compassion for others when thinking about yourself.
- A person cannot be easily provoked and operate in the Spirit's gifts and administrations.
- You cannot be provoked because it will knock you out of it, which happens all the time when God is about to use you.
- Afterwards you look back and think *that was a setup* because satan knew God would use you, and he was trying to knock you out of the Spirit.

What keeps you from loving others?

____

____

____

____

❖ I see this happen all the time. I have to be very careful about who I talk to and who I am around right before I minister because there are all kinds of things that happen to try to knock you out.

- You cannot be provoked, and you cannot be self-seeking.
- You have to be thinking of others.
- You cannot be provoked or overly sensitive and easily angered.
- If you are ministering by the Spirit and you are walking in love, you have to be able to stay in love.

❖ In Chapters 12 and 14 of 1 Corinthians, Paul talks about the gifts of the Spirit, and he throws Chapter 13 in because he knows the warfare we will go through.

- Paul is talking about building up the church because satan does not want that to happen.
- As he is writing Chapter 13, he is thinking about the things that are going to attack a person and cause them not to operate in these manifestations or giftings of the Spirit.
- He is telling them, "You cannot demand your own way. You cannot be self-seeking. You cannot get easily provoked."
- "You cannot be overly sensitive, and you cannot take into account the wrong that has been done to you."
- "You cannot keep a record of the wrongs."

- If your gifting is prophecy, you have to be aware that the reason you have that gift is that you are going to speak forth, minister, and build someone else up in the body.
- It is not selfish. It is not something for yourself.
- You have to be careful that you are not self-seeking, or it will knock you out of walking in that gift.
- You cannot be rude.

What can separate you from operating in your giftings?

____

____

____

____

❖ You cannot be provoked because it will pull you out of the Spirit, and then your gift will not operate correctly because you are provoked.

- You cannot be overly sensitive or angered, or you will be thinking about that instead of digging down deep inside.
- You have to walk in love and flow from that depth.
- You cannot take into account a wrong. You have to let that go.

- What if God has a word that has to do with someone who has offended you? You have to get that right because you must minister from the Spirit.
- The Spirit wants you to say a specific thing or minister to this person, but if you are keeping track of wrongs or being overly sensitive, it will prevent you from operating in these gifts effectively.

What causes you to stay effective in your giftings?

____

____

____

____

❖ **<u>1 Corinthians 13:6 NLT:</u>**

It does not rejoice about injustice but rejoices whenever the truth wins out.

- Paul shows us here how we should respond in the way we live.
- We do not rejoice in injustice, and we do not get excited when something unjustly happens.
- We rejoice whenever the truth prevails.
- The Holy Spirit wants to manifest in all the gifts.

- When you go to prophesy, you are prophesying His truth, which brings justice. We want the truth to prevail.
- When you speak from love, you want the truth to triumph and come out from that area of love.
- You want justice to come from that truth and prevail in that person, and you rejoice in that.
- If you are offended by that person and want something wrong to happen to them, that is the wrong spirit.
- You cannot operate in the wrong spirit because then you are just a clanging cymbal.
- You cannot prophesy correctly from love if you are offended or have unforgiveness.

In what does love rejoice?

____

____

____

____

❖ **<u>1 Corinthians 13:7 NLT:</u>**

Love never gives up, never loses faith, is always hopeful, and endures through every circumstance.

- Paul goes even deeper in this verse as if it wasn't hard enough about rejoicing in the truth.
- You should never be happy when something bad happens to someone because it is the devil who kills, steals, and destroys. You cannot rejoice in injustice.
- Jesus wants to give life and life more abundantly (John 10:10).
- You should be happy only when truth prevails.
- God is love. Perfect love drives out fear because fear has to do with torment (1 John 4:18).
- Love never loses faith, and it never gives up.
- It is the same with other people. You never give up on them.
- Until your last breath on earth, never give up. Always press in.
- Always pray, believe, and prevail, never losing faith.
- Stay in there, and never give up.
- That is perfect love.

What is Paul saying are the characteristics of love in this verse?

____

____

____

____

DISCUSSION:

When you are prophesying, and there are interruptions, or the power goes out, and there is no sound on the microphone, just keep prophesying. If the devil wants to shut down a sound system, my faith kicks in even more. I will not lose faith. I am going to get very bold and continue. I will never give up, and I will finish my message. I remember one time I was preaching in New Jersey and talking about the Lord's holiness, the holy fire, and the holy sapphire. As soon as I mentioned the holy fire, the lights went out in the church. It went out in most of the city of Newark. It was out until the very next morning. I finished my sermon that night after an hour and ten minutes in the dark without a microphone because there were so many people there. I knew the devil wanted to stop me, so I would not give up. When I got there the next morning, the power still wasn't on. It eventually came back on at a certain point before the service started, but I was ready to preach my whole sermon again no matter the circumstance because I will never give up.

❖ Perfect love does not lose faith and is always hopeful.

- When things happen, you will carefully choose your words and continue to speak from hope, even if you have difficulty believing.
- It will cause you to be more effective in the gifts of the Spirit.
- With prophecy, you might be saying something that is so hard to say, but you cannot speak from your circumstances.

- Prophecy is speaking from God's perspective.
- It is speaking what God wants.
- You are looking at the situation, and even though you do not think it could ever happen—you still have to say it because that is what God wants.
- God wants justice all the time.
- He wants you to prophesy that people will stop doing terrible things in the world.
- It may continue to happen tomorrow even though you spoke out what God wanted.
- These things need to be said because God is a just God.
- Sometimes they are hard to say, but they still need to be said.

What is required of you to speak from God's perspective and not your circumstances?

____

____

____

____

❖ Jonah did not want to minister to the people of Nineveh. He went in the opposite direction. The people of Nineveh were terrible people. They were very cruel terrorists and were well known for it. Jonah thought at first that he would not go there because he was afraid they would kill him. He obeyed God anyway because he knew that they would be judged and that ultimately was why he went. It was not out of love. To his surprise, the people repented, and he was mad that they did. He was not a prophet that was walking in love, nor was he rejoicing with their repentance. He was not excited that justice and truth reigned when people heard God's message and repented, and he was mad.

- God wants to help you endure through every circumstance.
- He does that by perfecting you in love.
- You are going to endure the hardships and be hopeful.
- Love endures all things and bears up under every circumstance.
- Regardless of what comes, you are going to stay in there.
- Even when it looks like it's not going to happen, stay in there.
- The Amplified Version of 1 Corinthians 13:7 in Greek says that love hopes all things [remaining steadfast during difficult times], endures all things [without weakening].
- Love is hopeful, remains steadfast in difficult times, and does not weaken.

How has Paul's definition of love changed the way you will conform to love?

____

____

____

____

❖ **1 Corinthians 13:8 NLT:**

Prophecy and speaking in unknown languages and special knowledge will become useless. But love will last forever!

- People have said that tongues have ceased because of this verse.
- They said prophecy and speaking in tongues have come to nothing or will end, and love will last forever.
- We know that Paul is talking about building up the body.
- According to Ephesians Chapter 4, all these gifts are to be used to build up the body into the unity of the faith.
- Until we are unified in faith, and we come to maturity, or until we come into perfection.
- In other words, we are perfected in our faith or perfected in love.
- That has not happened yet, so you cannot say that all the gifts of the Spirit have ended. We have not reached perfection yet.

- Paul is saying these will end, and we will not need prophecy at a certain point.
- We will not need tongues or all the gifts of the Spirit because there is coming a time when we are in perfection, as in Heaven.
- When I was in Heaven, I did not need a word of knowledge, tongues, or the gifts of Spirit. They are not needed up there.
- You are in perfection, and you have arrived. You do not need to be built up anymore. You are there, and that's the way it is.
- Down here on the earth, we need a word of knowledge or a word of wisdom. We need tongues and interpretation and prophecy.
- We need those manifestations through individuals coming and ministering to us.

What is the goal of the gifts of the Spirit?

____

____

____

____

❖ **1 Corinthians 13:9 NLT:**

Now our knowledge is partial and incomplete, and even the gift of prophecy reveals only part of the whole picture!

- There will come a time when love will last forever, and all prophecies will pass away.
- Tongues will cease, and the gift of knowledge will pass away.
- Paul says that we are partial right now and incomplete, but there is coming a time when we will be complete.
- All the cessationists and people who say the gifts of the Spirit are done, and the apostles and the prophets are done are taking this verse out of context.
- Paul is saying that until these things are perfected, we need to walk in love.
- We need to have knowledge because our knowledge is partial and incomplete.
- Even the gift of prophecy reveals only a part of the whole picture, so we know in part, and it is fragmentary.
- When perfection comes, these partial things are going to become useless.
- We are not at perfection yet, and that is why we need prophecy, the gifts of the spirit, speaking in tongues, and we need to build ourselves up in the most holy faith.
- Paul isn't saying that this has ceased. He is saying a time will come, and we are not there yet.
- We have prophetic perspective, and this is the sequence of the prophetic.

- We are following the sequence of revelation to the very end and finding where we are now.
- That is why a generation is coming up that will prophesy from the fire of God.

When will prophecy and tongues pass away?

____

____

____

____

CHAPTER 10

Maturing The Body of Believers

But you, dear friends, must build each other up in your most holy faith, pray in the power of the Holy Spirit.
—Jude 20 NLT

DISCUSSION:
The Spirit of God wants to manifest through all the gifts of the Spirit. If we are not perfect, the Holy Spirit will want to perfect us by building us up in our most holy faith while praying in tongues. We need to be built up in all the gifts. All those with the word of wisdom, and word of knowledge, need to operate in their giftings to confirm and give words from the Spirit. We need people to pray in tongues and interpret over us. We are not in perfection, and we have the gifts because everyone needs help. The gifts of the Spirit and the fruits of the Spirit are going to operate, and we are going to need them until we reach perfection, and that is the goal. It has not happened yet, but we are at the end of time when the bride is supposed to be spotless—without spot or wrinkle. At the end of the age, Jesus will come and get His bride.

❖ **1 Corinthians 13:10 NLT:**

But when the time of perfection comes, these partial things will become useless.

- The Spirit is causing all of us on earth to operate in our giftings by the Spirit.
- When perfection comes, everything that was partial and incomplete will be gone. It will all pass away.
- At that point, you will not need certain things like healing because you will be perfected in your body, your mind, and your Spirit in Heaven.
- You will have a new body because there is no sickness in Heaven, and there is no poverty or lack in Heaven.
- You will know things by the Spirit, and there will be no hindrances. All of these things will pass away, and we will not need any of them, but for now, we do.

How will you operate and steward your giftings on earth until you reach perfection? What is the purpose of the giftings given?

____

____

____

____

What happens when you get to Heaven?

____

____

____

____

MATURING THE BRETHREN

❖ **1 Corinthians 13:11 NLT:**

When I was a child, I spoke and thought and reasoned as a child. But when I grew up, I put away childish things.

- Paul talks here about the body of Christ maturing.
- It is like children who are becoming adults and do not have the same needs anymore.
- They have understanding and begin to participate as an outflow instead of always being in need.
- The time we are in right now is that we need to develop in maturity to be history makers by giving and providing answers and solutions in the Spirit.
- We want to be those that provide manifestations of the Spirit.

Instead of being needy, what are you becoming?

____

____

____

____

❖ **1 Corinthians 13:12 NLT:**

Now we see things imperfectly, like puzzling reflections in a mirror, but then we will see everything with perfect clarity. All that I know now is partial and incomplete, but then I will know everything completely, just as God now knows me completely.

- We can look around and see that things are not perfect
- We are in a broken world, and it is "like puzzling reflections in a mirror, but then we will see everything with perfect clarity."
- Paul is saying that it is like a blurry mirror down here.
- You cannot see your reflection clearly, but one day you will.
- When I prophesy and speak in tongues or pray in the Spirit, there are no limitations.
- I go to that other place in the future, and you can do that right now by praying in tongues.
- Your Spirit is praying, and there is no concept of time.

DISCUSSION:

I saw this on the other side when I died. I saw clearly, and I understood clearly, and I did not need to pray in tongues. I did not need a word. I saw everything, and it was perfect. When I pray in the Spirit now or when I prophesy, it's like my spirit goes back there, and I pray from this timeless realm where I am already in Heaven. I feel like I am in the future prophesying. I am getting people to come in line, but I am speaking from the future. I feel like I am prophesying and telling people, "This is what is ahead and what God wants; just keep on this path." I always want to prophesy from the Heavenly realm. I always want to say, "I am seated with Christ," I don't want to prophesy from down here. I need to go into the other realm and speak to the earth and the people from that place.

Where are you prophesying from? How will your prayer life change when you know where you are praying from?

____

____

____

____

FULLY KNOWN AND KNOWING FULLY

- ❖ One day we will see Him, and He will be perfect. We will be face to face with Him, and there will be no distance.

- Even though we know in part like fragments, we will know fully.
- Right now, we have to pray in tongues and interpret.
- We have to have words of knowledge, words of wisdom, and discerning of spirits. We see things, but we do not see everything.
- We have the pursuit of God where we want to understand Him and know Him. Therefore, we pursue Him.
- We search the Scriptures and allow the Spirit to counsel us, but one day we will know Him and be known by Him.
- We are already known, and I saw this when I was in Heaven.
- I saw that it is not easy for a person to excel and mature down here because of the onslaught of the enemy.
- You have to be diligent to be fully known.
- You must know it in your spirit and know you can be transformed. Your mind can be transformed (Romans 12:2).
- You can renew your mind and get there.
- You can get to a place where you know that you know, and you are fully known.

Why do we pray in tongues? Why must we be in maturity?

____

____

____

____

- ❖ You have to get to a point where you know God hears you. He already knows your next step and wants to take care of everything. When things happen that are contrary, you have to hold your peace and know that God is taking care of it.

    - When you pray in the Spirit and prophesy, you are bringing the other realm into this realm and bringing correction.
    - It is causing you to operate in the future.
    - What you are saying in the Spirit is the absolute truth.
    - We are told in Romans 8:26 that when you talk about praying in the Spirit, you do not know what you should pray, but the Spirit prays for you and intercedes for you with words that you cannot even know or express.
    - When you pray in the Spirit, the Spirit prays the perfect will of God.
    - That will of God is futuristic, and until you do this, you will not know what the will of God is.
    - You do not even know how to pray, but the Spirit steps in, lifts you up in your weakness, and super intercedes for you.
    - The Spirit is calling the things that are not as though they are (Romans 4:17).

How is it that you can keep your peace in the midst of difficulty?

____

____

____

____

DISCUSSION:

I have had people tell me that they knew the language I was praying in tongues. Once when I was praying, they said the Spirit is calling out names and places, and they will all happen within 24 hours. They said, "By 5:00 p.m. tomorrow, all these things are going to happen." They were impossible things and even geographically impossible. However, the next day I found myself there at exactly 5:00 p.m., and all these things happened, including meeting certain people spoken by the Spirit. If I did not have someone who knew the tongues I was speaking and spoke that native language fluently, I would not have known what the Spirit was saying. That was foreknowledge. It was the future, and the Spirit was reading it off like a schedule. This experience happened back in 1985, and it was an amazing time. I remember the guy being so surprised when he heard me fluently speaking in his language, but he was telling me what was going to happen next, and then it would happen. I realized that we are fully known by God, and we can know Him. However, we might need a shift in understanding to see that God knows everything ahead of time.

❖ God wants to tell us everything, and He is not holding anything back.

- God is not preventing you from anything.
- He is not preventing you from having enough money.
- He is not preventing you from having enough time to do everything you need to accomplish all He has called you to do.
- God will not tell you to do something and not give you the provision or the time to do it. He wants to help you.
- All the hindrances you have down here are because of the enemy.
- On the contrary, the Spirit is saying you will succeed—the Spirit is always willing. He always wants to accomplish God's will.

How will you approach praying in tongues now, and how has your perspective changed?

____

____

____

____

❖ Even though God's will does not always happen in your life, it will improve.

- You will get more accurate and start to abide in Him.

- That is the goal of the Spirit of God inside you. It is to be fully known and to know.
- The Spirit of God wants to get you to that place.
- He wants you to yield so that you can operate in the gifts of the Spirit for others.
- It is so that you can speak to them and bring them into being fully known, to walk in the future by the Spirit.
- You can expect impossible things to happen, knowing they will happen because you have prayed them out.
- Once you have prayed them out, you will begin to prophesy them out. You will begin to speak impossible things from the Spirit.
- You will say it in the known language and call those things that are not as though they were. That is what God did.
- He made things out of nothing. He called things that were not as though they were.
- He made the worlds by words. He spoke it out, and it came to pass.

Where does the Spirit of God want you to arrive?

____

____

____

____

What is His main purpose for operating in the gifts of the Spirit?

____

____

____

____

❖ **<u>1 Corinthians 13:13 NLT:</u>**

Three things will last forever—faith, hope, and love—and the greatest of these is love.

- This is unselfish love.
- This is the confident expectation for hope, abiding in this trust that God will fulfill His promises. All of this will happen for you.
- God operates through all the gifts. He operates by love. He wants everyone to operate in prophecy.

THE UNITY OF THE SPIRIT

❖ **<u>Ephesians 4:1 NLT:</u>**

Therefore I, a prisoner for serving the Lord, beg you to lead a life worthy of your calling, for you have been called by God

DISCUSSION:

Paul talks about being a prisoner of the Lord and starts with this dialogue with the church of Ephesus, and he explains how you operate every day in the Spirit. If you can do these things, you will be able to prophesy so easily. You will not have to shift into the Spirit. Many people live carnally, and because of that, they have to shift into being spiritual, but that is not the way it is in Heaven, and it certainly is not that way in the Scriptures. You are a spiritual person and live in a body, but your body is in submission to you. You tell your body what to do and tell your mind what to think. Your spirit is the strong one.

- ❖ Paul proclaims that he is a prisoner of the Lord and wants you to appeal to a life worthy of your calling.

    - In order to prophesy and operate in the gifts of the Spirit, living a life worthy of your calling has to become second nature to you.
    - If you are doing carnal things, grieving the Spirit, or not feeding yourself spiritually, you will not be ready and will have to shift.
    - If you live from the Spirit all the time, you can go to the marketplace, be at your job, acquire business success, minister by the Spirit and never have to shift into the Spirit.
    - You can feed the poor, minister at your church, or do a Bible study, and you will never have to shift gears, and you can learn how to do that.

How do you live a life worthy of your calling?

____

____

____

____

- ❖ Paul wants it to be known that he is a prisoner of the Lord. He is declaring that he has been captured and incarcerated by the Lord. His life is not his own anymore. That is true Christianity, and it will cause you to be effective and operate in the gifts of the Spirit.

  - Paul sets an example for you to live a life worthy of the calling. He is not just talking to the prophets or apostles; he is talking to the congregation at Ephesus.
  - He says to live a life that exhibits good Godly character, moral courage, personal integrity, and mature behavior.
  - A life that expresses gratitude to God for your salvation.
  - It is not enough that you are saved and have the gifts of Spirit.
  - Your life should exhibit Godliness.
  - You set an example as an imitator of God (Ephesians 5:1).
  - Paul is talking about personal integrity and mature behavior.
  - Living your life this way expresses gratitude toward God.

- Your behavior and the way you live tell God, *thank you.*
- God sees it this way, but it is not being taught.
- It will help you so that you can prophesy on the spot because there is no carnality in you.
- You do not have to shift and think or act in a certain way. You do not go in and out of this.
- As a Christian, you are always supposed to be in the Spirit. Your life expresses thankfulness to God.

How do you lead a Godly life?

____

____

____

____

❖ **Ephesians 4:2-3 AMP**

with all humility [forsaking self-righteousness], and gentleness [maintaining self-control], with patience, bearing with one another in [unselfish] love. Make every effort to keep the oneness of the Spirit in the bond of peace [each individual working together to make the whole successful].

- All of this is part of walking in the Spirit.

- The main thing is operating in unselfish love toward one another.
- You are helping others to look good as well.

According to Ephesians 4:2-3, what is the purpose of keeping the bond of peace?

____

____

____

____

❖ **<u>Ephesians 4:4-8 AMP:</u>**

There is one body [of believers] and one Spirit--just as you were called to one hope when called [to salvation] —one Lord, one faith, one baptism, one God and Father of us all who is [sovereign] over all and [working] through all and [living] in all. Yet grace [God's undeserved favor] was given to each one of us [not indiscriminately, but in different ways] in proportion to the measure of Christ's [rich and abundant] gift. Therefore it says, "WHEN HE ASCENDED ON HIGH, HE LED CAPTIVITY CAPTIVE, AND HE BESTOWED GIFTS ON MEN"

- Grace is the undeserved favor given to each of us in different ways in proportion to the measure of Christ's rich and abundant gift.

- Jesus was in the belly of the earth and ascended on high, but He took captivity captive.
- He took back everything that was stolen, took it with Him, and bestowed gifts to men.
- He took everything that was supposed to be for man, that was lost in the garden, and He bestowed gifts to men.
- He gave the gifts of the Spirit, our inheritance, and everything we lost in the fall back to us.

What did God do to render what was stolen from man?

____

____

____

____

❖ **Ephesians 4:9-10 AMP:**

(Now this *expression*, "He ascended," what does it mean except that He also had *previously* descended [from the heights of heaven] into the lower parts of the earth? He who descended is the *very* same as He who also has ascended high above all the heavens, that He [His presence] might fill all things [that is, the whole universe]).

- Jesus went down to the belly of the earth, and He took with Him captivity. He took all the loot and took it up.
- Everything that was stolen He distributed back to men that He may fill all things—that is, the whole universe.

❖ **Ephesians 4:11-13 AMP:**

And [His gifts to the church were varied and] He Himself appointed some as apostles [special messengers, representatives], some as prophets [who speak a new message from God to the people], some as evangelists [who spread the good news of salvation], and some as pastors and teachers [to shepherd and guide and instruct], [and He did this] to fully equip *and* perfect the saints (God's people) for works of service, to build up the body of Christ [the church]; until we all reach oneness in the faith and in the knowledge of the Son of God, [growing spiritually] to become a mature believer, reaching to the measure of the fullness of Christ [manifesting His spiritual completeness and exercising our spiritual gifts in unity].

- The five-fold is to build everyone up so that they are perfected in service to build up the body of Christ.
- Here is the complete summation of prophecy. Each gift of the Spirit that people can operate in is for this template right here.

- We are supposed to build everyone up spiritually.
- We are to grow people up until we reach oneness in the faith and until we reach the full knowledge of the Son of God.
- We can manifest this spiritual completeness through exercising our spiritual gifts.

Why did God appoint the five-fold to equip the saints according to Ephesians 4:11-13?

____

____

____

____

❖ **<u>Ephesians 4:14-16 AMP:</u>**

So that we are no longer children [spiritually immature], tossed back and forth [like ships on a stormy sea] and carried about by every wind of [shifting] doctrine, by the cunning *and* trickery of [unscrupulous] men, by the deceitful scheming of people ready to do anything [for personal profit]. But speaking the truth in love [in all things—both our speech and our lives expressing His truth], let us grow up in all *things* into Him [following His example] who is the Head—Christ. From Him the whole body [the church, in all its various parts], joined and knitted *firmly* together by what every joint supplies, when each part is working properly, causes the body to grow *and* mature, building itself up in [unselfish] love.

- Paul instructs us that we are no longer children.
- We are spiritually mature,
- You can prophesy and speak forth all the mysteries, but your life must also match those words.
- When you prophesy, you must live by your prophecy, even though you are prophesying to someone else or the body.
- You will have to listen to your own message.
- You have to take that prophecy, make it your life, and live by it so that other people can see the prophecy by how you live.
- We speak the truth in love both in our speech and in the way that we express the truth through our lives.

According to Ephesians 4:14-16, what does God want to do by equipping and maturing the saints?

____

____

____

____

❖ If only you could see the plan that God has for man on the other side and how it is perfect the way Jesus came and redeemed us.

- Our part is to walk in the power of the Spirit and be used by Him.
- We must allow ourselves to get out of the way by transforming our minds. That way, it permits God to have His way.
- We do not want any hindrances, so we yield and allow the Spirit to not only use us in the gifts but cause us to be mature enough to operate in them fluently in whatever way He wants.
- You should always have a word.
- Every time that you go somewhere, you should be ready.
- You should be built up in the Spirit by praying in the Spirit and have understanding.
- The Spirit is saying something to you in your understanding.
- You are not just building yourself up in tongues, but you have something substantial that you can share. Then you go forth.

DISCUSSION:

I am always waiting, and it is not always about going somewhere. Sometimes the Lord will tell me that someone is going to call and that I should take their call, and He will tell me what to say to them. It may take two to three hours, but they eventually call, and I will have a word for them. It happens every single day. I will be talking to people and giving them a word. It is not always obvious, but this is the operation of the Spirit in these last days. I encourage you to build yourself up by praying in the Holy Spirit.

- Study a certain subject or a verse and meditate on it all day. Let the Spirit begin to counsel you.
- God will give you a platform, and you will prophesy it, teach it, counsel people, and share it, but it will be from the fire. It will be from prophecy.
- It will come out like fire, and it should happen every day.

It happens to me several times a day. I am constantly getting words and getting ready. When I teach, I give out words all the time. I am not calling individuals up because it will be for the whole body. I will prophesy to the whole body rather than just pull individuals up because I can be more effective, and the Spirit can do more in everyone if I keep it corporate. Remember that God always reroutes your life so that you can minister. He always does that and will tell you how you will do it. He will say, "Today we are going to say this, or today, we will come from this approach. We will walk in love. We will not be offended." If I told you how many times the Lord said, "You are going to minister to this person," and that person did everything that day to try to offend me and get me knocked out, but I stayed in and never gave up on them. By the end of the day, I delivered the Word of the Lord. The devil was trying to knock me out and not walk in love, so be aware of how demons work.

How will you cultivate your life by the Spirit so that you are ready in season and out of season?

____

____

____

____

❖ **Remember the key points that we learned in this study guide:**

- You have to be full of the Word of God in your heart and mind to be good at prophesying.
- You should always be building yourself up in the Spirit and praying in the Spirit.
- You have got to be able to prophesy from the fire and be unhindered. Your character has to be developed.
- You have to be patient, you have to be bold, and you have to be able to deliver the word as though you are a prophet, just like the prophets of old.
- You deliver that word no matter what it is.
- Remember to build yourself up in your most holy of faith.

- Know the Word of God, and have the character that you can deliver that word at any moment, whether it be in the marketplace or a Bible study, wherever you are.
- You have always got to be ready.

List some key points you learned from this study:

____

____

____

____

Map out a faith plan centered around a relationship with Father God that you wish to fulfill:

____

____

____

____

SALVATION PRAYER

Lord God,
I confess that I am a sinner.
I confess that I need Your Son, Jesus.
Please forgive me in His name.
Lord Jesus, I believe You died for me and that You
are alive and listening to me now.
I now turn from my sins and welcome
You into my heart. Come and take control of my life.
Make me the kind of person You want me to be.
Now, fill me with Your Holy Spirit, who will show me how to live for
You.
I acknowledge You before men as my Savior and my Lord.
In Jesus' name. Amen.

If you prayed this prayer, please contact us at
info@kevinzadai.com for more information and material.

We welcome you to join our network at
Warriornotes.tv for access to exclusive
programming

To enroll in our ministry school, go to:
Warriornotesschool.com

Visit KevinZadai.com for additional ministry materials

About Dr. Kevin Zadai

Kevin Zadai, Th.D., was called to the ministry at the age of ten. He attended Central Bible College in Springfield, Missouri, where he received a Bachelor of Arts in theology. Later, he received training in missions at Rhema Bible College and a Th. D. at Primus University. Dr. Kevin L. Zadai is dedicated to training Christians to live and operate in two realms at once— the supernatural and the natural. At age 31, Kevin met Jesus, got a second chance at life, and received a revelation that he could not fail because it's all rigged in our favor! Kevin holds a commercial pilot license and is retired from Southwest Airlines after twenty-nine years as a flight attendant. Kevin is the founder and president of Warrior Notes School of Ministry. He and his lovely wife, Kathi, reside in New Orleans, Louisiana.

Other Books and Study Guides By Dr. Kevin Zadai

Kevin has written over fifty books and study guides Please see our website for a complete list of materials! Kevinzadai.com

60-Day Healing Devotional

60-Day Devotional: Encountering the Heavenly Sapphire

60-Day Devotional: The Holy Spirit

60-Day Devotional: Supernatural Finances

The Agenda of Angels

The Agenda of Angels Study Guide

A Meeting Place with God, The Heavenly Encounters Series Volume

Days of Heaven on Earth

Days of Heaven on Earth: A Study Guide to the Days Ahead

Days of Heaven on Earth Prayer and Confession Guide

Encountering God's Normal

Encountering God's Normal: Study Guide

Encountering God's Will

Encountering the Heavenly Sapphire Study Guide

From Breakthrough to Overthrow: Study Guide

Have you Been to the Altar Lately?

Heavenly Visitation

Heavenly Visitation: Study Guide

Heavenly Visitation Prayer and Confession Guide

How to Minister to the Sick: Study Guide

It's Rigged in Your Favor

It's all Rigged in Your Favor: Study Guide

It's Time to Take Back Our Country

Lord Help Me to Understand Myself: Study Guide

Mystery of the Power Words

Mystery of the Power Words: Study Guide

The Notes of a Warrior: The Secrets of Spiritual Warfare Volume 1 Study Guide

The Notes of a Warrior: The Secrets of Spiritual Warfare Volume 2 Study Guide

The Power of Creative Worship: Study Guide

Prayer Nations With Kevin & Kathi Zadai

Praying from the Heavenly Realms

Praying from the Heavenly Realms: Study Guide

Precious Blood of Jesus: Study Guide

Receiving from Heaven

Receiving from Heaven: Study Guide

Spiritual Discernment: Study Guide

Stories from the Glory with Sister Ruth Carneal

Supernatural Finances

Supernatural Finances Study Guide

Supernatural Prayer Strategies of a Warrior: Study Guide

Taking a Stand Against the Enemy

Taking Off the Limitations

Taking Off the Limitations: Study Guide

The Vision and Battle Strategies of Warrior Notes Intl.

Warrior Fellowships Season 1 Volume 1 Study Guide

Warrior Fellowships Season 1 Volume 2 Study Guide

Warrior Notes Aviation Volume 1: Flight Manual Study Guide

Warrior Women Volume 1 Study Guide

Warrior Women Volume 2 Study Guide

Warrior Justice: A Study Guide to Experiencing Freedom from Demonic Oppression

You Can Hear God's Voice

You Can Hear God's Voice: Study Guide

Made in the USA
Middletown, DE
24 August 2022

72093362R00124